SCREEN SMARTS

A Family Guide to Media Literacy

SCREEN SMARTS

A Family Guide to Media Literacy

Gloria DeGaetano and **Kathleen Bander**

Best Wishes —
Gloria DeGaetano

HOUGHTON MIFFLIN COMPANY Boston New York 1996

For information about this and other Houghton Mifflin trade and reference books and multimedia products, visit The Bookstore at Houghton Mifflin on the World Wide Web at http://www.hmco.com/trade/.

Library of Congress Cataloging-in-Publication Data
DeGaetano, Gloria.
Screen smarts : a family guide to media literacy / Gloria DeGaetano and Kathleen Bander.
p. cm.
Includes bibliographical references and index.
ISBN 0-395-71550-4
1. Mass media and the family. 2. Mass media and children.
I. Bander, Kathleen. II. Title.
P94.5.F34D44 1996
306.85 — dc20 95-42682
CIP

Printed in the United States of America

QUM 10 9 8 7 6 5 4 3 2 1

For my sons,
precious beyond words.

—GDG

For all the children I've ever known . . .
and for my father, who steered me by example.

— KB

Acknowledgments

We wish to thank the following individuals for their unstinting support throughout the process of writing this book:

Elizabeth Wales, our literary agent extraordinaire, who validated our experiences and enthusiastically joined in our efforts to reach a broader audience;

Dr. Jane Healy, whose selfless dedication to children and parents has been an inspiration for us;

Dr. Katharine Heintz-Knowles, who offered needed encouragement so that this project could get off the ground;

Dr. George Gerbner, for inspiring us with his pioneering work in media literacy;

Our colleagues and friends, especially Gail Mitchell, Dianna Slack, and Lynn Haney, whose attentive listening helped focus us and whose heartfelt support sustained us;

And especially, David Moore and Bill Mirand, our husbands, who know the symptoms of overload, how to relieve them, and who gave needed encouragement and timely suggestions.

Contents

Foreword

In an era when an increasing variety of media seeps ever more seductively into our lives, parents and teachers retain a singularly ambiguous relationship with visual technology. On the one hand, we willingly acknowledge that it won't go away, and, in fact, that most of us can't live without it. Yet we continue to regard products of the flickering screen with suspicion and even distaste—particularly as it gains a tenacious hold on the minds and emotional lives of our children.

Such wariness is justified. Although most research on the effects of television on children is funded by program producers, thus rendering the results less than fully credible, the few unbiased studies that have been conducted suggest that excessive and unsupervised viewing and video game–playing may have profoundly harmful effects. Most concerned parents have already figured this out; the problem lies in how to separate their glassy-eyed progeny from the delights of mental downtime and the titillation of inappropriate content.

As programming and formats grow more sophisticated and more enticing (often through visual and technical tricks that are not apparent to the average viewer), a battle for the control of youngsters' minds intensifies. Many parents tell me that they try unsuccessfully to limit type and quantity of viewing; the younger generation, meanwhile, asserts its sense of entitlement to participate in whatever looks like fun in the adult world. The result is a growing generational rift that escalates the normal rebellion of the young into alarming proportions. I have addressed large audiences of earnest parents whose anxiety level over how to manage the media was palpable; I have also heard from hundreds of teachers who knew that the chasm between the values of the school and those of the media culture are so at odds as to alienate a large majority of students from serious concern about matters academic. The survival of literacy, not to mention the quality of our future culture, appears to be in jeopardy.

Into this maelstrom of conflicting interests come Gloria DeGaetano and Kathleen Bander, two teachers who understand how to speak directly to the needs of real people. Here they offer us field-tested techniques for helping children learn to make viewing time a learning experience. "As a society," they remind us, "we are taught how to read and write, but we have never been taught about visual images—how they work, how they affect us, and how we can use them for our purposes."

Is it possible that watching TV might make you more, rather than less, literate? Although these authors spell out in clear detail the potential hazards of too much unsupervised "screen time," they do not advocate unplugging. Rather, they urge us to the new discipline of media literacy—meeting the monster head on and subduing it through knowledge and critical evaluation. In the process, they answer many questions that plague today's parents: "How much time should my child spend watching TV and playing video games? How can I intervene without ruining my relationship with my child? Is computer time better than TV watching? How do I select suitable programs and/or software?" Most important, they present practical and accessible pointers for improving family time (and, quite possibly, everyone's IQ) by emphasizing the importance of discussing programs that have been viewed and analyzing the devices used by producers to manipulate audience reaction.

The concept of media literacy is not widely known, but it is prime time for exploring its potential. Our children will have access to increasingly powerful and pervasive visual images. They will need them in the workplace and they will rely on them for entertainment. Why not teach them how to manage their own viewing habits and reactions so as to retain control over this medium? Children can learn to see vacuous content, stereotypical characters, bias, and manipulation for what they are. They can learn to appreciate and actively support good programming while rejecting the dross. As the world becomes increasingly media driven, it is our responsibility as parents to give our children a new set of survival skills, those of media literacy.

Jane M. Healy, Ph.D.
August 1995

Introduction: Raising Media-Literate Children

The little screen flickered at long last as anticipation grew in our living rooms. It was the early 1950s, and we were about to experience something that seemed like a miracle. We didn't know it at the time, but the introduction of television to the American family was to drastically change the way we lived. It would come to transform our entire society.

Television watching rapidly became the main family "activity." Each and every night, right after dinner, parents tuned in. Children watched, too—after-school shows like *Howdy Doody, The Mickey Mouse Club, Superman,* and *The Lone Ranger.* Family time that had been spent in conversation, playing games, or in other activities diminished or evaporated. Television—an intriguing new invention—was beginning to entrance us.

Today, video screens greet us everywhere we go: in airport terminals and on planes; at child-care centers; in classrooms and in museums; at major sports events; in restaurants; in health clubs; at our local library and our favorite department store. Adding to television's visual impact are the newer screen technologies—computer and video games, virtual reality, superhighways, and information retrieval systems. From the tiniest hand-held video game to the all-enveloping sights and sounds of the modern movie theater, the lure of the screen beckons us in ways unimaginable forty years ago.

Yet, as much as we've come to enjoy media images, we have also learned to respect their power. Can we doubt the impact of visual images? Remember the triumph we felt as a nation as we watched the first steps being taken on the moon? Or how the newsreel footage of the assassination of President John F. Kennedy kept us glued to the screen as we sought to make sense of that tragedy? Think of the devastating images of the Vietnam War that projected night after night from our living room screens, generating our disenchantment with our country's role there. Today we know what we couldn't have known in the fifties—that screen technology is more than an information and entertainment device: it is a formidable agent of social change.

Children are particularly vulnerable to the power of visual technologies. In blatant and in subtle forms, media messages alter the way children think about themselves and the world. Consider these statistics: A television is on in the average American home seven hours a day; more than 60 percent of American families watch it while they eat their evening meal;[1] by age eighteen, kids will have spent *twice as much time* in front of a screen than they will have spent in twelve years of classroom instruction;[2] by the time they enter kindergarten, preschoolers will have spent more time watching TV than a college student spends in four years of classes.[3] Over an eighteen-year period, the accumulated time children spend in front of visual screens, including television, video and computer games, rented videos, and movies in the theater, is staggering.

Most parents have strong hunches that too much television and video watching is not good for children, but the reasons why are not always obvious. In this book we discuss how, specifically, excessive TV and video watching impacts children's growth and the measures that parents can take to guide their children's development in a media age. We have found that with this type of detailed information, parents are better equipped to deal proactively with television and video in their families.

Gloria DeGaetano has been involved in public education for more than twenty years. She has been a classroom teacher, a reading specialist, a school district administrator, and a university instructor. In 1985 she was working with teachers on successful models of classroom learning, and she became curious about how television viewing at home was impacting children in the classroom. She also wanted to learn how excessive TV watching could affect her own two young sons. She began her research thinking she would finish in two weeks and pass on the information to her colleagues. Two years later she found herself still digging through dusty library shelves, compiling research from a variety of disciplines. What she found impressed her so much that she changed jobs and began working full-time in the area of media literacy. She has since shared much of the information in this book with hundreds of parents and teachers through her highly acclaimed lectures and workshops.

After years of work in public relations and television production, Kathleen Bander became a classroom teacher. Inclined to dismiss the statistic that the average child watches anywhere from four to six hours of television a day, she decided to put it to the test and asked her students to report both how much and what they watched. She was disturbed to find that the statistic was true. She also observed that though the students knew very little about the hows and whys of television, when they were given this information, they soaked it up enthusiastically. To this end, Kathleen developed a parent-assisted curriculum that taught children the basics of media literacy. Parents found this so helpful that Kathleen looked for further relevant materials for them, but found very few. This prompted her desire to develop a more comprehensive tool for parents. Her research led her to Gloria, and the idea for this book was born.

Teaching children media literacy skills will take time and a good deal of effort. But in an age when a single screen is used for computer games, global correspondence, and watching the latest Hollywood movie, it is increasingly important that kids learn to evaluate visual images. Media literacy skills also enhance other areas of learning, such as language development, communication, and critical thinking.

As a society, we are taught how to read and write, but we are not taught about visual images—how they work, how they affect us, and how we can use them for our purposes. However, this world of visual technology requires that we all become media literate. This means that we carefully choose how we are going to use visual technology in our lives, that we consciously choose how much of it we use, and that we scrupulously evaluate what we do use. And we must impart to our children that their own creativity, their own ideas and abilities, are as significant as the ones they see on the screen every day. To teach children how to critically analyze all visual technologies is to give them powerful tools that will equip them to succeed in the twenty-first century.

SCREEN SMARTS

A Family Guide to Media Literacy

1

As Children Grow: Screen Influence

Imagine for a moment that it's twenty years from now and you are enjoying lunch with your child, now an adult. As you sit across the table from your son or daughter, who are you seeing? What are you observing about this person you have lovingly raised? Is she energetic, healthy, and happy? Interesting to talk with? Is he a good problem-solver? What about his confidence level? Her creativity? Is your son or daughter basically a capable adult?

While we parents may not know specifically what we want our children to be doing in the nebulous future, we do know some general characteristics we would like them to have as adults. Most of us would agree that we want our kids to grow up to be happy; with a solid sense of self-worth. We would like them to use their skills and talents in creative, productive ways; to be contributing members of society; to be kind to others and themselves. We want them to think before acting; to be motivated to learn new things; to have a fulfilling life; to teach *their* children well.

For these reasons, parents strive to choose capable child-care providers, to make sure homework is completed, and to conference with teachers. When time permits, many of us might coach our children's teams, drive carpools, attend PTA meetings, and throw birthday parties. In the midst of this whirlwind, we may not often consider the adult our child will become. The present demands too much of our attention. But if we stop and think about it, we may want to pat ourselves on the back for all we do to help our kids grow up sound and healthy.

Children are faced with certain tasks that they must complete during specific stages of their development; accomplishing these tasks ensures proper body and brain growth. Child development experts call these tasks Mother Nature's imperatives because they are crucial for children's optimal growth.

Heeding Mother Nature's Imperatives

What Mother Nature couldn't foresee was the complexity in guiding children to achieve age-specific knowledge in a video world. Too much time spent watching TV may interfere with developmental tasks and hinder growing bodies and minds. Visual technology, unharnessed, can cloud the vision we have of our children as competent adults.

However, television and video can support and enhance our children's growth—the trick is to use them wisely and at the appropriate time in a child's life. The rules of the game are very different for a fourteen-year-old than they are for a four-year-old. An understanding of human development can help put TV and video in perspective, with our children's needs at the forefront. What happens or doesn't happen during childhood and adolescence determines, to a large extent, who an individual becomes.

In this chapter we examine the needs of the child's developing body and growing brain. Then we look at the effects of excessive television watching on children and adolescents by providing a detailed discussion of the important developmental tasks in three age categories: birth through age five; ages six through eleven; and ages twelve through fourteen.

The Developing Human Body

Overuse of the TV screen frequently means underuse of young cardiovascular systems. To develop healthy hearts, lungs, and muscles, children need regular exercise. There is a high level of concern among health professionals that in this age of technology, children are more out of shape than ever before.

For instance, the American Academy of Pediatrics issued a report revealing that "up to 50 percent of school-age children are not getting enough exercise to develop healthy hearts and lungs, and that 40 percent of youngsters between ages five and eight exhibit one risk factor for heart disease."[1] The academy believes that too much time in front of the TV set is a major contributor to this state of affairs.[2]

Realizing the urgency of the problem, the American Heart Association launched major campaigns to call attention to children's need for more physical activity. Their public service announcements "Caution: Children Not at Play" and "Remember When 'Play' Was More Than a Button on the VCR?" have appeared in national magazines to call the public's attention to the issue.

Scientific studies conducted in the past decade have shown that children who spend many hours watching TV and playing video games are likely to be overweight and to become adults with health problems such as high blood pressure, obesity, and diabetes. In a study of 1,097 children, researchers at the University of California found that those children who watch two or more hours of TV daily are at increased risk of having high cholesterol levels when they become adults. The risk climbs the more they watch. The study concluded that many of these children could have dangerously high levels of cholesterol in later life.[3]

As most of us know, it doesn't take much for the hours children spend in front of screens to add up—an hour before school watching cartoons, an hour after school playing video games, two hours in the evening watching TV with the family. A few days or even several weeks at this pace wouldn't be worrisome—it's the cumulative effects over a span of many years that take their toll on our children's health.

The Human Brain

The human brain simultaneously coordinates and integrates our instincts, feelings, and thinking functions. Some researchers have described three different clusters of brain structures that seem to work together to orchestrate this delicate balance. The lower brain, sometimes referred to as the "reptilian system," plays a large role in controlling instinctual responses, in physical coordination, and in self-preservation. The "limbic system," or "middle brain," seems to play a significant role in mediating feeling states. The cerebral cortex, or

Remember When "Play" Was More Than A Button On The VCR?

Send your kids out to play. It'll help them establish life-long exercise habits that may lower their risk of heart disease as adults. *You can help prevent heart disease and stroke. We can tell you how. Call 1-800-AHA-USA1.*

This space provided as a public service. ©1994, American Heart Association

Reproduced with permission. "Remember When 'Play' Was More Than A Button On The VCR?" Winter/Spring 1994 PSA Ad Kit, 1993. Copyright © American Heart Association.

"higher brain," plays a dominant role in our ability to think, to create, to make decisions, and to experience self-understanding.

Childhood is a critical time for the growth and integration of brain functions. However, when television and video use become habitual for children, appropriate brain development may be threatened. Important functions may not develop optimally because excessive viewing time displaces time the child needs to spend in tactile exploration of the sensory world, in using and listening to complex language structures, and in working through difficult problems to reach solutions.

The Developing Brain Requires Tactile Experiences As well as strengthening the growing body, physical activity in childhood builds the mo-

Reproduced with permission. "Caution: Children Not at Play," Winter/Spring 1992 PSA Ad Kit, 1992. Copyright © American Heart Association.

tor control centers in the low brain areas, ensuring proper large- and small-muscle coordination and developing a mature sensory motor system, necessary for accurately perceiving and processing incoming data.

Many tactile experiences, such as sand and water play, art projects, block building, and cooking are essential for developing the low-brain areas, providing the critical foundation for future higher brain functioning. Kids with a TV habit are losing opportunities for these types of sensory-rich 3-D experiences. Looking at two-dimensional screen images is very different from actually being involved in the world; watching a nature show is treated differently by the brain than hiking through the woods. Although the content of television varies,

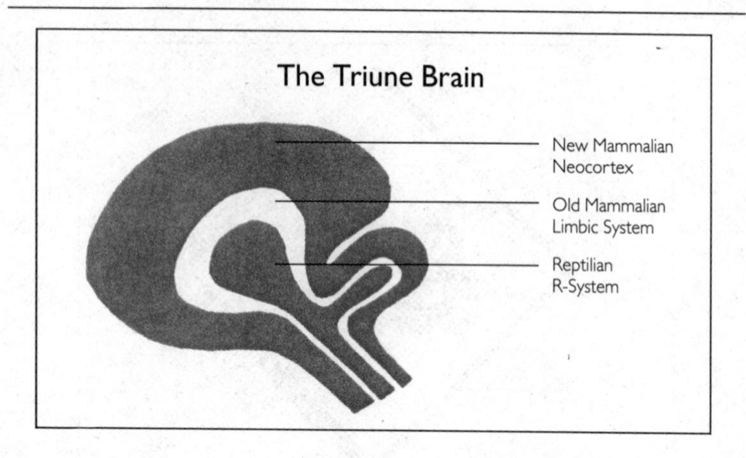

the experience is the same. Images on a screen, no matter how exciting and colorful, do not encourage sensory motor system capacities. Viewing is not doing. Tactile experiences lost throughout childhood are difficult to replace later on.

The Developing Brain Requires Symbolic Processing Functions Our current societal shift from pencil and paper to the visual screen has been compared to ancient Greece's shift from oral storytelling to the newer forms of reading and writing. In light of how the human brain functions, this analogy is not at all accurate.

The Greeks made a transition from oral language, a brain activity requiring symbolic processing, to written language, another brain activity requiring symbolic processing. Although aspects of long-term memory were lost when the oral tradition was lost, the human cerebral cortex continued to master higher forms of abstract thought.

Today, as children passively watch moving images, they are making a transition *away* from symbolic processing. Visual images on a screen are immediately accessible. As Dr. Russell Harter, who studies the relationship between television and the developing brain, points out, "Television . . . is not very symbolic. It makes things easy to understand."[4]

Language, on the other hand, whether oral or written, requires cogitation; because of its symbolic nature, its meaning must be unlocked. Words on a computer screen are processed by the brain very differently from pictures on the same screen. And what is potentially harmful to children is the displacement of talking, reading, and writing by the viewing of images. Why? Because symbolic processing (using language skills) is the critical prerequisite for advanced thinking abilities. In fact, there is no thought without language or some type of abstract system, such as sign language. Try thinking without language and see what we mean!

Many people today conclude that the visual nature of our information age is changing the way our kids think. However, thinking about a visual image still requires the same rigorous brain activity as thinking about an essay or other printed material. The picture, without symbolic processing, only gives the illusion that one has knowledge. It takes analysis and interpretation to make sense out of visual messages. These brain processes are best developed in the child through language—talking, listening, reading, and writing. Think of the cart and horse analogy: Visual images are the cart; language the horse. Language must come first, before the child's brain is saturated with visual images; otherwise the brain's ability to think critically will likely be harmed. A society that doesn't recognize the relationship between language and thinking abilities inadvertently hinders its children's cognitive development, risking their future success. In reality, the age of the visual screen is not changing *how* children think so much as it is changing *whether* they think.

The Developing Brain Requires Mental Challenges Have you ever wondered why educational programs don't draw as wide an audience as the fast-paced, violent ones do? Much of it has to do with how the brain functions. Fast-moving screen action triggers instincts and requires little thought to get its message across. The cerebral cortex doesn't operate as fast as the other brain systems, and rapid-fire images don't allow much time for the cerebral cortex to engage, to formulate ideas. Therefore, an educational television program requires more concentration and mental effort, especially for a child, whose cortical functioning is not fully developed. We'll discuss this point in more detail in Chapter 3, when we explain the draw of media violence.

A child's brain depends upon continual mental challenge for growth. Dr. Marian Diamond, professor of anatomy and director of

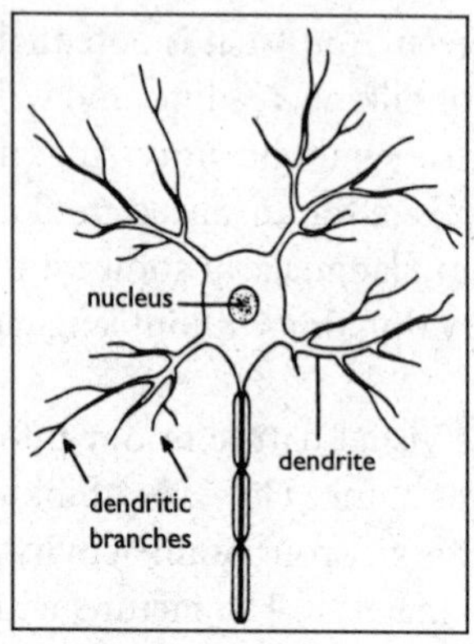

Neuron with few dendrites

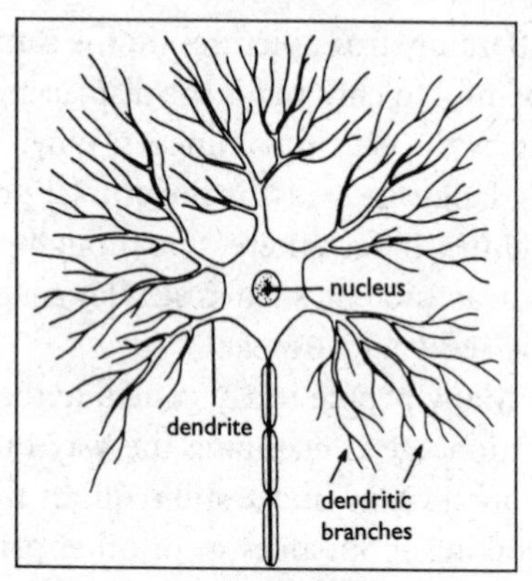

Neuron with many dendrites, which can result from long-term exposure to intellectual challenges

the Lawrence Hall of Science at the University of California, has found that the structure of cells in the brain's cortex physically changes as a result of sustained intellectual exercise, with individual neurons developing more connective links (dendritic branches) to other neurons.[5] In other words, when the brain is used for thinking, it can actually grow more mass. On the other hand, if the child's brain doesn't apply specific thinking functions often enough, those functions will not mature. By allowing children unlimited access to visual technologies while demanding less time in challenging activities, such as reading or solving puzzles, parents unintentionally contribute to a state of mental deprivation—which may seriously affect the rate and quality of a child's brain development.

It is, however, possible to use TV and video to support children's cognitive development. By discussing TV programs with children—by asking thoughtful questions and presenting mental challenges—parents will nurture both language and thinking abilities.

Ages and Stages of Growth

At different ages, children's brains require varying stimuli. The next section examines the most critical developmental tasks. This information may help you make parental decisions about TV, video, and computers for children and teens.

From Birth through Age Five

Marcy is an experienced, yet frustrated, preschool teacher. Every year she encounters an increasing number of youngsters who don't have the skills she knows are necessary for learning. And in the few hours she sees the children every week, she can't fill in all the developmental holes. Marcy says:

> It used to be, say ten years ago, that I would have three or four children who required special attention. But today, it's more like twenty-three or twenty-four. Something is terribly wrong. These youngsters have extremely delayed language and cognitive skills, attention spans of only several seconds, no imaginations. Many of them have never been read to, have no knowledge of basic games, and have never put together a simple puzzle. What they do have, though, is a wealth of knowledge about video games, TV, and movies—most of it totally inappropriate for their age.

Marcy isn't alone in voicing this concern; early childhood educators nationwide are observing similar patterns. The more time spent in front of TV, the less capable the youngsters seem to be. For appropriate development in early childhood, nothing—not even the best quality screen program—can take the place of rolling in the mud or snuggling with a bedtime story.

The four basic tasks of young children, outlined below, provide the crucial foundation for a lifetime of successful learning.

Multisensory Play Early childhood is a time of discovery and exploration. Exasperated parents of toddlers will lament, "They are into *everything*." And well they should be, however trying their wanderings are. Active play such as making sandcastles, water play, drawing with crayons and paints, building with bristle and wooden blocks, molding dough, and creative play with puppets and stuffed animals engage most or all of the child's senses.

Sensory deprivation may occur when there is too much screen

time and not enough real-life play. In extreme cases, over a period of years, sensory deprivation can atrophy the senses and distance children from their intuitive natures.

Television limits sensory input because it requires only sight and sound, with an emphasis on sight. When one or two senses are overstimulated and the others have little or no stimulation, the central nervous system "revs up"—it becomes overloaded—and seeks release. This can result in hyperactivity or the zoned-out effect that we see after a child has watched too much television or spent too many hours playing video games. Young children are especially vulnerable to sensory deprivation when they are in front of screens for prolonged periods without adult guidance.

More time in multisensory play and less time in front of a screen will develop sensory acuteness, which enables proper brain functioning. For, in reality, it is our senses that provide the brain with information. As Diane Ackerman reminds us in *A Natural History of the Senses,* "The brain is silent, the brain is dark, the brain tastes nothing, the brain hears nothing. All it receives are electrical impulses—not the sumptuous chocolate melting sweetly, not the oboe solo like the flight of a bird ... not the pastels of peach and lavender at sunset over a coral reef—just impulses. The brain is blind, deaf, dumb, unfeeling."[6]

Without a well-functioning sensory motor system, then, the brain is at a great disadvantage. The best time to build this all-important system is in early childhood. And nothing does the job better than play, which requires the use of all or most of a child's senses. For this reason, many experts discourage excessive time on computers at preschool, because this prevents youngsters from being actively engaged with their surroundings.

Language and Thinking Development In early childhood, networks for language ability are also growing rapidly. In this visual world of ours, parents cannot go wrong by establishing a regular routine of reading aloud to young children. The earlier the better, since research suggests that habits established in early childhood will likely continue as children grow older. By listening and focusing on beautiful language structures from a book such as *The Velveteen Rabbit,* the child begins to learn how to concentrate and how to think. Children can listen to language several years beyond what they themselves can speak, read, or write. At the moment, they may not be able to give a full account of what was read, but eventually the words, phrases, and ideas from the books will become part of the child's oral vocabulary and written language. When educators see a four-year-old being read to on a consistent basis, they applaud because they know that that child at fourteen will have strong communication and thinking skills, will more likely be a great reader, and will be a capable if not gifted writer. *There is no easier way to ensure children's future learning success and problem-solving abilities than by reading aloud to them.*

The language on TV does not build the child's linguistic capacities for several reasons: the language is not complex enough; the visual images get in the way; and the TV can't respond to the child—it can't ask or answer a question or slow down to give the child time to absorb what's being said.

When a child listens to a story, many activities are occurring inside the brain: The brain is working to make sense of the words, phrases, and sentences, to turn them into ideas. The child is activating her own visual imagination. She is learning how to focus and concentrate her attention on complex language and ideas. She is responding to the narrative, figuring out what makes a story a story. She is learning new vocabulary, new ways of expressing herself, and new ways of seeing her world. These "brain gymnastics" are invaluable, and they are best learned at this stage of child development.

Listening to language is so important for little ones that parents should consider investing in a cassette player and obtaining story tapes from the local library for additional language input. With a little practice, young children will sit and listen to a story on audiotape by themselves. Four- and five-year-olds will enjoy learning how to use the tape recorder and can become independent in their choice of stories. When parents need a break, are busy putting dinner on the table, or just want the child to sit quietly for a while, a good option is to set the child up with a story tape rather than in front of the television set. In the course of a week, preschoolers should be spending as much or more time listening to stories read aloud than they do watching TV or playing computer or video games.

Creative Play A distinct characteristic of this age is playing "Let's pre-

20 Reasons to Read Aloud to Your Child

1. It develops a child's listening skills.
2. It activates the imagination.
3. It provides interesting family conversation topics.
4. It provides important language modeling.
5. It develops a child's ability to think critically.
6. It enhances a child's ability to think symbolically.
7. It stimulates writing abilities.
8. It's fun!
9. It's an inexpensive form of entertainment.
10. It increases a child's attention span.
11. It provides a peaceful family activity.
12. It develops a child's desire to read.
13. It models a rewarding lifelong habit.
14. It gives a child the sense of language rhythm.
15. It helps to pattern neural pathways that are developing.
16. It expands a child's vocabulary.
17. It increases a child's ability to concentrate.
18. It gives a child needed practice in predicting information.
19. It expands a child's world view.
20. It's the single most important thing a parent can do to help a child succeed in school.

tend." Young children benefit greatly from unstructured, creative play. It nurtures their imaginations, provides opportunities to model adult language and behaviors, and teaches them cooperation and negotiation if they are playing with friends. Today, however, children too often merely imitate what they see on the screen in their creative play. For instance, many educators have observed that youngsters who are overexposed to screen images tend to repeat the stereotyped scripts from cartoons or movies and do little to expand plots and settings or invent new characters. It isn't wrong or unusual that children borrow ideas from cartoons or other shows for their activities. But

Imaginative vs. Imitative Play

Imaginative Play

Child uses materials at hand: Child uses empty boxes, kitchen utensils, leaves and twigs, and other various materials, which take on magical properties and are transformed to suit the child's needs at any given moment.

Child creates new roles: One day the child is a gardener, the next a bus driver, the next a scientist. Some days, a cartoon character. Roles are varied and represent a wide context of the child's daily living experiences.

Child generates own language: Codes, secret words, and special names are integral parts of self-controlled, self-directed play.

Child develops a variety of play scenarios: Child combines real experiences with vicarious experiences to form varied, colorful, elaborate themes and settings.

Child uses generative imagination: Child uses bits and pieces from books, TV, and life to weave an original, creative play experience.

Imitative Play

Child uses icon toys: Toys are ready-made and reproduce cartoon characters or media personalities, reinforcing screen messages and values.

Child repeats stereotyped roles: Day in and day out, the latest screen images are the dominant, or only, roles for creative play.

Child repeats scripts or sound bites: Child uses stunted screen language. In fact, original plots or creative twists are not easily accepted.

Child imitates TV scenes: Child uses only screen images as a source for play ideas and scenarios.

Child uses memory recall: Child uses memory to imitate what is seen on the screen, with little or no use of own imagination.

Using Books to Help Preschoolers Expand Ideas for Creative Play

- ❑ Buy or make several puppets, name them after your child's favorite book characters, then have your child be one puppet while you be the other. Discuss events from the book, make up a different ending, add new scenes, change characters' personalities—have fun letting the puppets act out your child's version of the book.
- ❑ Read books that relate to some aspect of your child's imaginative play. For instance, if your child has been including the cat in some of his escapades, you may want to get some fiction and nonfiction books about cats. David McPhail's *The Big Cat* is a good place to start!
- ❑ Keep a treasure box near your reading place and have your child fill it with favorite toys. You may want to add some clothes and other props. When you read a story aloud, have your child pick items from the treasure box and use them to help her act out the story.
- ❑ Let your child pretend to be the author of his current favorite book. Talk with him about what an author does and then ask him questions about how he came up with the ideas in "his" book.
- ❑ Read books by the same author and make up a special "circle of friends"—a group of characters from the author's books that your child especially likes. Then have your child make up adventures about her circle of friends and act them out using props from the treasure box. She could also dictate stories to you about these characters, which you write down and later read aloud to her.

when the television becomes the *only* source for ideas, children's play becomes more imitative than imaginative.

Imaginative play has specific characteristics and is the natural propensity of the young child. In the chart on page 13, notice the distinct differences between imaginative and imitative play.

Parents can encourage a broader range of play topics by exposing children to different experiences, diverse settings, new people, unusual foods, and interesting books. With encouragement, young children will use their impressions of these experiences to create a variety of scenarios and characters in their play. Parents can also guide children in expanding imaginative possibilities.

Using books is a good way to expand children's play into more imaginative realms, to make their play more personal, original, and creative. Jane decided that while she read aloud to her two- and four-year-old sons, she would occasionally have them act out the plot of the story. For instance, when she read *No Place for a Goat,* a story about a goat who comes to a house and eats his way through it, one of her sons played the goat and the other played the woman with the broom chasing the goat. The children loved acting this out, for this was the one time it was acceptable to jump on the couch! They wanted to have the book read over and over again. In the following weeks, Jane noticed that her sons had incorporated some of the ideas from *No Place for a Goat* into their play. She was so encouraged by the fact that her boys were interested in something other than G.I. Joe that she resolved to read more books to them more often and let them act out the stories. It was a great success.

Another mother, Sally, told us she had a brainstorm one night when fretting over her five-year-old son's fascination with war play. Since Power Ranger action figures were the only toys he wanted to play with, she invited him to bring them along to bake cookies and to garden. She even encouraged him to give the Rangers regular bubble baths. It wasn't long before her son ascribed different personality traits and sentiments than aggression and hostility to his action figures.

Unstructured, Nondirective Play "I'm bored." How often do parents hear this lament? It can trigger in us a sense of duty to *do* something about it—*now.* "Well, honey, why not help me write this letter to Grandma?" "No." "Wouldn't you like to color?" "No." "What about getting your blocks out?" "No." And on it goes. If we get lucky, we finally suggest something our child will want to do. On unlucky days, the frustration builds, making a usually peaceful time with our children an unwanted hassle. When young children say they are bored,

To foster children's growth from birth through age five, parents can:

- ❑ Provide opportunities for multisensory-rich play.
- ❑ Read aloud often and/or provide story audiocassettes.
- ❑ Encourage creative play by providing a variety of clothes for dress-up, cardboard boxes, paper, crayons, paint, and other useful tools.
- ❑ See that daily time is spent in nondirective play by making sure that your child is not overly scheduled.
- ❑ Balance the time your youngster spends in front of a screen with time spent engaged in activities.

one tack is to say: "O.K., just stay bored until you figure out what to do." "What?" "That's right. Just sit on the couch, think, stare into space, and wait until an idea comes to you."

Young children can be taught early on that it's O.K. to be bored, it's O.K. to not know what to do every minute, and that it's O.K. to figure out what they want to do by themselves, without mom or dad's help. Sitting and staring out the window, lying in a pile of autumn leaves looking up at the sky, playing with the puppy, just being ... these types of activities allow your child to wonder about the world and wander within himself.

Parents can support this need by providing regular opportunities for nondirective play. It is important to avoid filling up the child's time so that she has the chance to come up with her own ideas about what to do—children are naturally inventive when we give them time and space to invent. When parents give a child room to breathe, the pots and pans soon are out of the cupboard and she's building a city with them, or the restless five-year-old has confidently decided he will record the sounds he hears around him, starting with his barking dog.

It certainly is tempting to fill children's spare time with TV and video. It's a simple solution, and they are sure to be entertained.

However, when screen images are used to keep a preschooler occupied as part of the daily routine, the child does not learn how to entertain herself. In fact, a certain laziness can easily set in. Flicking on the button can become the antidote to struggling with the question, "What is there to do next?" By avoiding this impulse, you will help your children learn the power of their own ability to look inside themselves and figure it out. Young children who have more experience in the "fertile void" are more likely to grow into adults who are capable of using their talents and skills to the fullest. Or, as the poet Eve Merriam put it, "It takes a lot of slow to grow."[7]

Ages Six through Eleven

Dan is a veteran fourth grade teacher in a large suburban school district. Recently he was given the opportunity to teach a different grade, but he opted to stay where he was because he enjoys the nine- and ten-year-old age group. He loves his work, but is concerned that he isn't able to address all of his students' needs—many are still struggling with simple tasks. States Dan:

> Each year it gets worse. Many of my students don't enjoy reading and are several years below grade level. Many have poor study habits and are very difficult to motivate. I know TV isn't the only culprit, but it's got to be a significant factor. I took a survey recently and found that in my classroom of 31 students, the total number of TV sets owned by their families was 82—one family had 5 sets. Many kids had a TV in their bedrooms. In the survey, 86 percent admitted to watching four or more hours a day, and even more time on weekends, and 52 percent said they played video games at least one hour per day. When do they read? When do they study? The dog doesn't eat kids' homework nowadays because kids don't do their homework. It's the TV monster that gobbles up their learning time.

In elementary school, children should be developing their personal talents and their language, thinking, and study skills. Parents can immensely contribute to their children's school success by carefully monitoring the number of hours spent around visual media and making sure children devote much of their time to the five important tasks discussed below.

Learning How to Learn The elementary school years are a time of skill development and learning just what it takes to grasp new concepts. Parents should use this time to encourage new interests. No matter how mundane a new interest might seem to us; if the child is enthusiastic about learning it, it's best for the parent to run with it. This helps children become more secure and confident in themselves and their emerging abilities.

Learning how to comprehend new concepts is an essential skill that is developed during this stage. This includes learning how to focus attention and concentrate over an extended period of time, to use the imagination, to problem-solve and draw on the memory, and to "stick with it" through the difficult phases. This latter skill, which experts call vigilance, has been found wanting in school-age children who watch a good deal of television.[8] Without this crucial ability, future skill learning will be difficult and, at times, impossible, because during the development of any skill there are always instances when a child wants to give up. The task will simply look too overwhelming. Those children who have developed the ability to persevere will excel despite the difficult aspects of learning and will enjoy the exhilaration and self-respect that come with succeeding in difficult tasks.

The Habit of Physical Activity As the sensory motor system is developing, children benefit greatly from physical activities, such as sports, dance, and outdoor recreation. Potential couch potatoes typically want to move less the more they watch. One option for parents is to make it a household rule that children may watch TV or play video games only after they have spent some time in a physical activity. Reinforcing the value of regular exercise is well worth our efforts because a habit of physical activity established during this stage will pay lifetime dividends.

Literacy Skills Learning to read and write are monumental achievements for all children, regardless of the pace at which they learn. Parents can make these tasks easier for children by reading aloud to them regularly (this is vitally important for this age group, too), discussing the books read, and establishing a nightly "family silent reading time." Parents can also write little notes for their children to read, play word games with them, write down their children's own stories and

Reading and Writing around the House: Ways to Nurture Literacy

- One night every week, each family member remains silent for an hour or two. Instead of talking, write notes, type letters, hold up signs on which you have printed directions or questions. All responses must be written down. Help little ones write what they want to say, but spelling doesn't count — even for the adults! After some practice, the family can make up and play a treasure hunt game using only written language.
- Keep a running shopping list on the refrigerator door and encourage your child to add to it when she thinks of something the household needs.
- Occasionally read aloud to your child a selection from a book, newspaper, or periodical that you find moving or interesting in some way — a poem, a descriptive paragraph from a novel, an inspiring ending, or just a sentence you find artfully constructed. Encourage your child to share the same from his current reading materials.
- Compile a family joke book. Everyone writes down favorite jokes on sheets of paper over a period of time. Put in a ringed notebook. Children could illustrate it, also. Pick it up and read it when a lighthearted moment is called for.
- Provide an "author's space" somewhere in your home — a quiet corner with a table, writing equipment, or a PC if you have one. Encourage all family members to compose. Share original stories and poems with each other. Encourage children to share their creations with siblings, friends, and relatives. Have children write and illustrate stories as birthday and holiday presents.

read them aloud, and encourage children to write letters to relatives and friends.

Educational programs such as *Reading Rainbow* may help a child learn new vocabulary or spark an interest in reading about certain topics. But TV programs, no matter how educational, do not involve children directly in the necessary literacy processes. Clearly a child must spend considerable time reading and writing in order to learn how to read and write.

Learning about Self While children at these ages are involved in many activities, they also need a regular dose of quiet time. Solitary play, a time to reflect, helps the child develop a sense of who she is and provides opportunities to explore ideas and find original ways to solve problems. In addition, she learns to mull over questions such as: What do I like? How am I different from others? How am I the same? What are my special strengths? What are my interests?

When children are left alone and they spend their time watching TV, their attention is focused on an external image, which takes time away from meanderings within. Distance from other family members can be found by going to an empty room, the front porch, or the back yard. Encouraging children to have a special spot, such as a tree house, a hiding place under a table, or a tent in the yard, helps her learn to enjoy her own company.

The adult capacity to enjoy being alone indicates emotional maturity and a creative spirit. Bruno Bettelheim, a renowned child psychologist and educator, states, "The biographies of creative people of the past are full of [childhood] accounts of long hours they spent sitting by a river ... roaming through the woods with their faithful dogs or dreaming their own dreams ... developing an inner life, including fantasies and daydreams, it is one of the most constructive things a growing child can do."[9] With today's hectic living pace, it is important to schedule our children's solitude as part and parcel of other regular routines to make sure they don't miss out on this meaningful time of renewal and self-discovery.

Cooperation Cooperation and negotiation are important social skills to be developed in these childhood years. Participating in noncompetitive sports, role-playing to solve conflicts without resorting to physical harm, discussing problems, learning how to compromise,

To foster children's growth from ages six through eleven, parents can:

- Nurture new interests and encourage a wide range of skills and hobbies.
- Provide regular time for reading and writing; read aloud often (daily).
- Encourage daily physical activity in the form of outdoor play, sports, movement, or dance.
- Provide opportunities for quiet, alone time.
- Encourage activities that teach negotiation and cooperation.

and learning how to establish a middle ground are ways in which children learn the importance of social restraint and the benefits of cooperative behavior. Unfortunately, the acquisition of such skills is hindered by the viewing of violent TV programs and video games. Screen violence sends children inaccurate messages about how people effectively resolve conflicts, and in some cases it may contribute to aggressive behavior and bullying tactics.

Ages Twelve through Fourteen

The early teen years are those during which children confront the arduous task of sorting out "What is me?" and "What isn't me?" By experimenting with various behaviors, attitudes, and beliefs, the young teenager is learning her boundaries. Much like the four-year-old playing dress-up, she tries on different roles to see how they fit—"Does it feel right to be an athlete, a debater, a cheerleader? Or am I just doing it to please my friends or my parents?" "Should I continue with my piano lessons or take up the guitar?" "Can I keep both my high grade point average and my friends?" "Does being into rap, horror flicks, and popular fashion reflect my personal values?"

When teens are supported by parents, teachers, and other caring adults, these identity crises are usually smoother processes, although not without their struggles and tensions. Being a teen in our culture is made profoundly more difficult because of media role models, consumerism, and advertising that mercilessly barrages this age group. The influence of peer pressure to go along with the latest hyped trends is very real at this age, and most teens succumb to it, at least somewhat. The four tasks described below are critical for young people, not only for a strong self concept, but also for developing a sense of purpose in life, a feeling of relatedness to the world, and a capacity for mature intimacy. By guiding teens and remaining present and available throughout these potentially turbulent years, parents help their children become responsible, self-respecting adults.

Learning about Self and Others Early adolescence is a dynamic time of change, expansion, and learning about self and others. It is the time when thinking skills mature and the young adult becomes capable of high-level reasoning. It is also the time of putting the finishing touches on many of the essential learnings of the earlier stages.

During this period, skills continue to develop and expand. Yet in this TV culture of ours, there is a tendency for young teens to narrow their interests to the stereotyped images they see. Broadening their experiences can reap many rewards. For instance, if a favorite TV show is a sitcom portraying African Americans in stereotypical roles, parents should discuss the program with their child and then watch an educational video that realistically depicts African American history and culture. In this way, parents expand the child's awareness beyond the limited scope of the television program and encourage the child to become more reliant on other sources for information about the world.

Developing Higher-Level Thinking Skills In the late childhood and early teen years, portions of the brain are still developing—the corpus callosum and the prefrontal areas. The corpus callosum connects the two hemispheres of the cerebral cortex and aids the integration of the left and right brain hemispheres—in other words, it allows a human to use all of the brain's territory. The prefrontal areas enable higher-level thinking, such as planning and organizing, reflecting on ideas, problem solving, and an awareness of one's own thinking processes. Older children and teens must participate in activities that develop these brain areas. Exercises that challenge the teen to plan, design, and create something are ideal, such as research projects, simulation games, craft projects, drama, creating art, playing an instrument, and writing music or poetry. If the corpus callosum and the prefrontal areas of the brain are not fully developed, the consequence could be deficiencies in the ability to apply creative imagination to problem solving and to apply analysis and evaluation in decision making.

> In a 1992 study of fans of various cult shows, the television expert Joseph Franklin found that teenagers who were avid fans of *Gilligan's Island* scored significantly lower on their SATs, had lower GPAs in high school, and suffered from more weight problems than teens who did not regularly watch the show and who could not sing the *Gilligan's Island* theme in its entirety.[10]

Developing Language Skills Language input also promotes brain development. Listening to audiotapes of science fiction stories, old radio shows, and classic literature helps young adolescents fine-tune their concentration. It challenges them mentally, provides complex linguistic structures as models for their own writing, and exposes them to exciting new worlds. Encourage teens to read a wide range of material, from newspaper editorials to poetry to nonfiction.

Engaging your teen in regular discussions about his or her day and about books read and movies seen will go a long way to develop both sophisticated linguistic expression and mature thinking skills. Partaking in relaxed conversation at the dinner table is one way to accomplish this goal. Some families reserve one night a week when everyone stays at the dinner table to linger over a cup of coffee or dessert and talk. Because teenagers are busy with homework, extracurricular activities, and part-time jobs, these parents thought it important that all family members reserve the same night each week to catch up and spend some time together.

Another way that teens can sharpen their thinking and language skills is by practicing good study habits. A parent-monitored study routine will provide the time and structure that are necessary to complete homework assignments. Parents can help their children to take study time seriously by setting the stage for them. These guidelines will help parents establish a study routine:

- Provide a place that is free of distractions such as TV and radio—quiet is most conducive for study. Make sure the area is well lighted and that all family members recognize that the area is designated for studying.
- Encourage your child to take regular breaks. Forty-five minutes to an hour should be the maximum stretch of studying. A good break might include a snack and a short walk.
- Plan the week's study time in advance. When possible, help your child organize for upcoming tests or long assignments.
- Give lots of positive encouragement for homework completed in a timely and successful manner. Celebrate a good grade on an important test or a difficult book read and understood.
- You or another family member take phone calls for your teen during study time. It's important that your child is not interrupted.

Physical Self-Awareness Adolescent bodies undergo tremendous changes and many hormonal ups and downs. During this sensitive stage, vigorous physical activity helps kids stay in touch with their bodies and keeps them well conditioned and strong. Media images of the "perfect" male and female body only serve to make young teens more self-conscious. Emphasizing the value of fitness and strength helps to steer kids' attention toward the benefits of a healthy body and away from media-generated ideals. Participation in a variety of sports or outdoor recreations such as hiking and orienteering will help ease the stress brought on by rapidly changing bodies.

The Most Important Consideration: Each Child Is Unique

Every child undergoes three distinct stages of development. Each child progresses at his or her own pace. By observing our child's activities and interests, we can determine the amount and type of interaction with TV and video that will support development, not hinder it.

To foster children's growth from ages twelve through fourteen, parents can:

- ❑ Provide a variety of opportunities for teenagers to develop their skills and broaden their horizons with new experiences. Encourage teens to discover new interests.
- ❑ Every day, discuss topics that are important to your teen.
- ❑ Encourage reading and discuss ideas and topics in newspapers, poetry, fiction, and nonfiction.
- ❑ Promote fitness. Stress health, not image.

Sarah, aged three, watched one hour of *Sesame Street* in the morning, and the previous night she had watched *Beauty and the Beast.* In the afternoon, Sarah demands to see a new video. Her mother understands that Sarah is the type of child who is happy spending *hours* in front of the television set. Therefore, her mother determines that today Sarah will play with puzzles and blocks and spend time outdoors. For the evening, she plans to have Sarah listen to a story tape, and then she and her husband will play puppets with Sarah before bedtime. When a child demands to watch TV, this is a cue that the child is getting hooked, and direct intervention is in order.

Andy, aged ten, is an honor student who loves all kinds of sports. He has a paper route that keeps him busy after school. He is bright and mature for his age. One night Andy reads about a TV special on youth violence and gang behavior. Since his fourteen-year-old brother is given permission to watch it, Andy asks if he can see it also. His parents have taken the time to examine the content of the program, and they consider his request. The previous week, a police officer had spoken to Andy's class about gangs. While the TV program contains graphic material, they agree to let Andy watch it because it could reinforce what he learned in school. Andy's parents make an agreement with him: Dad will view the show with the boys and discuss it with them afterwards. Andy and his brother are encouraged to ask questions during and after the program about parts that are unclear or frightening. Also, Andy is expected to talk about the program's ideas and compare them with those he learned in school.

Andy's parents know the program is not appropriate for all ten-year-olds. However, they base their decision on the potential value of the program to help Andy learn important information.

Becky, aged thirteen, is in the habit of watching TV every day after school. Since both her parents work, she has the run of the house for two hours before dinner. It becomes obvious to Becky's parents that her soaps are becoming more important to her than her homework. When her report card arrives with several D's, her parents know that action is called for. They tell Becky that she must complete her homework before watching TV. But how can they enforce the rule? They discuss their concerns with Becky, and the three reach a compromise: Becky can watch one favorite show after school, but then she must turn off the TV and begin her homework. If she finishes before dinner, she can watch TV later with the family. Becky likes this compromise and starts paying more attention to her schoolwork. She doesn't feel deprived and still is able to discuss her favorite show with her friends at school.

When parents base decisions about TV and video on how they will impact children's learning needs, a new family relationship with the media emerges. Then, rather than a hindrance, TV and video become useful tools for supporting and shaping our children's development.

2

A New Approach to the Home Screen: Family Media Literacy

Screens Are Not Neutral

Given the power of visual technologies, it is no surprise that we as a culture have come to accept them as great advancements. However, the shortcomings of any technology are not always obvious. This especially applies to television, video, and computers because they are respected in our society and have become integral to most of our lives. Jerry Mander, a social critic and long-time skeptic of television and video, notes that in the thousands of books written about television, no one has "thought to argue that we might be better off without it."[1]

Few of us are willing to refuse television and video altogether. Like the air around us, we take screen technologies for granted. As these technologies have invaded our lives, we have been tempted to allow them to shape our existence. This is particularly troublesome when it comes to children. Consider the following examples:

Janice is a PTA president and the mother of eight-year-old Kara. She works as an office assistant at Kara's school three days a week and occasionally volunteers in her daughter's third grade classroom. Diligent and involved, Janice expresses concern about what she feels are questionable practices at the school:

> Several of the teachers use videos as rewards so often that the children are now in the habit of expecting a video whenever they do any type of work. If this isn't bad enough, one of the teachers shows a video every day at lunchtime, rain or shine. Instead of encouraging the chil-

> dren to go outside and get some fresh air, they are enticed to stay inside and watch TV. It's gotten so that most kids don't go out anymore. Don't get me wrong—I'm not against video use in the classroom. But this overuse seems to be blatant irresponsibility on the part of the teachers and the principal. My daughter has seen more videos at school than she has at home.

Ned has been coaching Little League for nine years. He loves working with the kids and teaching them new skills. Over the years, Ned has observed something that gives him pause for thought:

> It's been a long-standing custom to hold a party to celebrate the end of each season. In the early days, we'd get together at someone's house for a potluck, the kids would play, the parents would talk, and then we'd all play some soccer or basketball. The kids always loved this. Toward the end of the party I'd give each child a certificate, along with some compliments for a job well done. Everyone would cheer and applaud each individual's efforts, and the kids beamed with pride as I rattled off their accomplishments. It was great.
>
> Today, things have really changed. The parents usually want to have the party at a pizza place so the kids can play video games after they eat. It's so noisy that no one can do much talking, and usually there's a big-screen TV blaring in the background and the kids are staring at it. Now when I give out the certificates, no one pays much attention. It's gotten so that I can't say a little speech about each of the kids anymore—they don't want to wait around and listen. They've got to get back to the video games. It's sad, isn't it?

Ellen is a teacher of developmentally delayed preschoolers. Recently she took a group of five-year-olds on a week's outing at a camp designed for special-needs children. Ellen was surprised and appalled at something that happened there:

> Every morning at breakfast, the staff would get the kids' attention by using a microphone, shouting songs and doing crazy antics, basically working the kids into a frenzy. It was ridiculous. These youngsters

need to learn to listen and could well do with some peace and quiet at mealtime so that the teachers at each table could carry on a conversation with them. Instead of using the time we had in nature to teach the children to pay attention, the staff hyped the kids up before they got their day started. It's as if people think we have to appeal to children like a busy video or we'll lose them.

Janice, Ned, and Ellen are expressing the weighty concerns of many parents and educators in this media age. The encroachment of the visual media is substantial, and it affects adults' assumptions about what children really need. For instance, because children spend a good deal of time in front of video screens, many adults—including teachers—believe that they must use the appeals and techniques of video to capture children's attention and interest. It is dangerous to assume that children need flashy, quick messages to be interested in learning new concepts; this type of erroneous thinking shortchanges children because the ways in which information can be displayed on a screen are limited.

The excessive use of the visual media can create a perpetual filter through which adults view what children need. Adults' assumptions that children are best served by video profoundly impact children's lives. At birthday parties, for example, the cultural norm is to watch a video as an expected party "activity." Children want it, adults think, so they provide it. Yet children who have never played party games are in a poor position to make any decision about what they like and don't like. Another example of the screen filter is the proliferation of video games, which are used to keep kids "entertained" in restaurants, airports, hair salons, and shopping malls.

Do adults think video games are the only form of entertainment that can hold children's attention? If children are given an alternative, they are likely to explore it. One enterprising company, Activities Unlimited of Louisiana, is supplying low-to-the-ground tables covered with Lego pieces in airport waiting areas across the country. Playing with Lego pieces better serves children's developmental needs than does playing video games, yet these types of opportunities that can truly benefit children are the exception, not the norm. In order to successfully meet all of children's play and learning needs, we must allow them to experience the fundamental and developmentally necessary activities of childhood.

Screens as Teaching Tools

Cheryl describes how she was raised with television:

> We had our TV in the kitchen and it was turned on a lot. But my mom was always talking back to it. Yelling sometimes, other times making jokes, especially about the commercials. It wasn't long before we kids started doing the same. I'll never forget the day that something really irked her. She happened to be canning tomatoes at the time and she started throwing them at the guy on TV. My brother and I picked up some tomatoes and started throwing them, too. It was great fun. Mom was considered a bit eccentric in her time, but she taught me a lot about how to deal with TV. During dinner the TV was never on, and we spent time talking about the shows we had watched in the afternoon, filling Dad in on all the details. Today I'm teaching *my* kids how to talk back to the television and the people they see on it—without throwing tomatoes, though.

By questioning TV's messages and talking back to it, Cheryl's mother was teaching her children important skills. Although her methods were somewhat unorthodox, this mother was ahead of her time. What Cheryl was learning as a child were the key components of media literacy.

Media Literacy

The word *literacy* connotes a high degree of competency. *Computer literacy* is the ability to use computers well; *print literacy* is the ability to use language well. *Media literacy* is the ability to use all forms of media well, including all visual technologies. A media-literate person uses television, movies, and video and computer games for specific purposes, just as a print-literate person reads a book or a magazine for a particular reason or with certain goals in mind. Instructing our children how to use screens intentionally is the first, and most important, element in teaching media literacy. Experts know that children who develop a video habit early on grow up less equipped to use visual technologies well. A media-literate person knows the differences between various forms of media and uses them appropriately. Just as a print-literate person can tell a fairy tale from a biography, a media-literate person knows the conventions of the different types of media. From sitcoms to docudramas to music videos to commercials, a media-literate person understands how different forms of media use various techniques to deliver their messages.

And just as a print-literate person knows how to read, a media-literate person also knows how to read. But instead of reading words, a media-literate person reads *images.* This entails interpreting the subtle messages of visual images through analysis and evaluation. With practice, it becomes second nature for a media-literate person to analyze the plot in a TV drama, compare the merits of two popular movies, understand how the images in a commercial are developed to evoke specific emotions, and to be wary of news that is delivered fast and furiously. Reading screen images involves the ability to understand the basics of how visual productions are made and how technical elements, such as lighting and camera angles, convey specific messages.

As with any skill, it takes time to learn media literacy. A media-literate person has the ability to reflect on, and, if appropriate, to act upon the content and influence of all forms of visual images, whether they are seen on the television, the computer, or the movie screen.

These are the basics of media literacy:

- *Use visual media consciously, not out of habit.* Make informed decisions about which TV programs and movies you watch. Balance your use of screen technologies with other life activities.
- *Critique the messages that visual images are sending.* Use analytical skills to examine visual messages.
- *Discuss screen images and their messages.* Communicate facts, ideas, and opinions about what you view.
- *Understand production techniques and how they influence visual messages.* All visual images are intended to convey specific

messages. A media-literate person can produce various forms of media—a school paper on a computer, a family history on video, a multimedia presentation for work.

Media Literacy Is Here to Stay

Media literacy is not a new concept in many parts of the world. In Great Britain and Australia, media literacy has been established as an integral component of the educational system for more than a decade. In Canada, groups such as the Association for Media Literacy in Ontario and the Canadian Association for Media Literacy in British Columbia have been pioneering the concept in schools, universities, and communities. In fact, most English-speaking countries are ahead of the United States in making media literacy education a top priority.

Diedre Downs, the executive director of the Downs Media Education Center, said, "With a media-literate population, we can think critically about and process all manner of information in a thoughful way. We can elevate our personal values and judge information without feeling threatened by it. We can make our own information and send it out into the world. . . . And best of all, we would no longer feel helpless or victimized by the vast legacy of the Age of Information."[2]

Across the United States, educators and legislators increasingly see media literacy as a critical skill for the twenty-first century; many teachers and librarians feel it is essential to children's academic success. Although schools in the United States have a long way to go in recognizing media literacy as an essential part of the curriculum, some inroads have been made in the past few years. One outstanding example is pioneer media educator Dr. Renee Hobbs's media literacy curriculum in the Billerica, Massachusetts, school system. This curriculum has gained the attention of the academic community, educational publishers, video manufacturers, and the popular media nationwide. Professor Hobbs aptly refers to media literacy as "a driver's training program for the information highway."[3]

Much of the success of the media literacy movement in the United States is due to the dedicated involvement of media artists across the country who teach kids how to make their own media. When children and teens stand behind the camera and look through the lens, they are less likely to be victimized by the visual images they see every day. One such media artist is Steve Goodman, the founder and executive director of New York's Educational Video Center (EVC), who has promoted the educational use of student-produced videos and has taught intructors production techniques that they can use in the classroom.[4]

The concept of media literacy is entering the mainstream, thanks to the efforts of several national organizations, such as the Los Angeles–based Center for Media Literacy. Established in 1989, the center is a leading publisher of media literacy educational materials for schools, churches, and community organizations, addressing such topics as sexism in the media, advertising, and media violence.[5]

These types of grassroots efforts on the part of individuals and organizations have resulted in the recognition by some states of the widespread need for media literacy education. On April 8, 1994, the mayor of Las Cruces, New Mexico, declared "Media Literacy Day" as part of a statewide program. *The National Media Literacy Project: Pilot State: New Mexico,* developed by the Downs Media Education Center, was strongly supported by the New Mexico Department of Education. It was a huge success. After one year of a broad-based media literacy campaign, tens of thousands of New Mexico citizens had an understanding of basic media literacy concepts, children were learning media literacy skills in school, and instructors were trained to teach media literacy in their classrooms.[6] Other states are taking action: North Carolina and Florida both have educational legislation promoting media literacy; California incorporates media literacy in its campaign against television violence; and Hawaii sees media literacy as an important way to prevent racism.[7]

Family Media Literacy

Becoming savvy about visual images can be an exciting journey for children. Even if media literacy skills are taught at school, they must be reinforced in the home. The value of parental supervision regarding TV and video has long been recognized by authorities. In fact, many experts agree that children are less apt to pick up screen misconceptions, imitate media violence, or model stereotypical behaviors commonly found on television when parents discuss screen messages with them and teach them how to analyze and evaluate these messages. Just as it is never too early for parents to start reading to their children, it is never too early to start educating them about television and video. Preschoolers can be taught to take control of the television and turn it off after a favorite program.

When we take the time to teach our kids media literacy skills, we are supporting their emotional and social development as well. Suppose you ask your five-year-old a few questions about her favorite show. She must reflect upon what she saw in order to respond to you. She practices language skills as she formulates her response, and she calls upon her ability to remember, to sequence events, and to compare and contrast ideas. She learns that it can be fun and stimulating to talk about the program she viewed with a caring adult; these conversations are rewarding intellectually and emotionally. She learns to value conversation as an important social skill while becoming more adept at it. She is grateful to have the undivided attention of someone who loves her, which encourages her to speak more often about the programs she watches.

The benefits are no less profound for the older child. Asking a twelve-year-old about a controversial film or television program encourages him to think critically, express himself articulately, and gain confidence in his own views. By eliciting and crediting his observations and thoughts, you convey to him that his ideas have worth. He may then learn to better understand and clarify his values, and may be motivated to talk with you more often.

Preparing for Family Media Literacy

Integrating media literacy into a regular family routine takes time, so incorporate the suggestions and activities in this book gradually. Try not to heap guilt on yourself for how you used TV in the past or if you think your family isn't progressing fast enough. It takes patience to learn new skills and new approaches to dealing with television and video. And it's never too late. At *any* stage of a child's or a teen's development, you will help your son or daughter immensely by taking even a few steps toward media literacy. Do what feels comfortable, comes naturally, and is fun for you and your family.

Since parents are the busiest people in the world, making media literacy a family priority does not need to be terribly time-consuming. But it does take some planning. To make media literacy an attainable family goal, we advocate the following:

- Set up your home to be a media-literate environment for children.
- Establish screen rules and strive for consistency.
- Plan use of screens ahead of time.
- Talk as you watch; keep basic questions handy.
- Encourage the three C's—communication, critical thinking, and creativity.

Set Up Your Home to Be a Media-Literate Environment for Children

In a real sense, the environment in which a child grows teaches the child. How accessible the television set is directly affects how much a child watches it. Many parents report that when the TV is placed out of the main traffic flow, they can more successfully keep viewing to a limit. If children must go out of their way to watch television, they may be more inclined to think through a decision to turn on the set and less likely to turn it on automatically.

Televisions, VCRs, and video game apparatus are showing up more often in children's bedrooms. While some kids may be able to use these wisely when they are so readily available, most kids cannot deal with the temptation. If a child is spending a good deal of time alone in her bedroom in front of a screen, she is not receiving the adult guidance necessary to become media literate.

Parents can do little things around the house to show their children that becoming media literate is a family priority, even when parents are not at home. Some ways include:

- *Put a sign on the TV set as a reminder for children.* Annie would not arrive home from work until several hours after her eleven-year-old got home from school. To make sure the TV remained off until homework was completed, Annie attached this sign to the front of the set: "Warning: If the TV is turned on before homework is done, allowance and privileges will be withheld." It became a ritual for Annie to check her son's homework when she got home from work. If all was well, then the TV could be turned on.

- *Keep a list of various activities handy so the TV isn't the only resource available.* An interesting story on cassette provides a viable, appealing alternative for children who come home to empty houses after school. A list of household chores, a new coloring book, or a few new books from the library are activities that invite learning and discovery. By giving children alternative options, you are encouraging them to be more discriminating in their choices.
- *Write questions about the child's favorite show on a card and keep it by the TV set.* Children are creatures of habit, and they enjoy watching a certain show at a specified time. Having a few questions planted nearby nudges the child's thought processes when a parent can't be available.

Establish Screen Rules and Strive for Consistency

It is important to establish family ground rules, for they give children structure and predictability. Most of the rules will focus on the frequency of screen use and should change as children grow older. Some examples of screen rules we've gathered from parents who rely on them for "household sanity" include:

- No TV or video games until homework is finished.
- No TV or video games before school.
- At least one night a week the television is turned off for a family activity.
- One week the television is on; one week the television is off.
- A certain number of hours are allotted for the week and the child determines what will be watched during those hours.
- A timer must be set by the person playing video games. When the timer goes off, it's time to quit.
- The daily total time watching TV, playing video games, and work-

ing at the computer must be less than the daily total time playing, reading, and doing homework and chores.

- The television must be turned off during dinner.
- The television must be turned off at a certain hour each evening.
- No TV on school nights.
- A weekly maximum, such as seven hours, for each family member.
- For every hour of television viewing, ten minutes are spent actively discussing what was watched.

When thinking about how much TV time to allow your child, keep in mind that the American Academy of Pediatrics has stated that one to two hours daily is the maximum time children should spend watching.[8] In considering the child and his or her needs, parents can use this advice as a starting point. Some children may be able to handle more TV or video time on occasion and some may need less time, depending on their age and stage of development.

Plan Use of Screens Ahead of Time

Planning ahead will alleviate hassles and free up time to spend in enjoyable family activities, rather than endlessly haggling over screen time and content. Both children and teens find it helpful to be able to predict when and for how long they will be allowed to watch TV and be involved with other screen activities. Some parents find it useful to post upcoming TV specials on a bulletin board or the refrigerator. They find that by alerting their children to an interesting show beforehand, it gives the family a chance to talk about the potential merits of the program, and the actual viewing of the show becomes more interesting.

Making a weekly TV schedule, for example, gives children a sense of structure and reduces the stress of determining "What do we watch tonight?" With TV or video choices planned ahead, that question has already been answered. To draw up a schedule, hold a family meeting on Sunday evening and go through a television guide for each day of the upcoming week. Use a yellow highlighter or a red pen to mark the programs your child will watch. Add up the cumulative time to make sure it is consistent with your goals for your child. Before choosing specific programs, discuss your child's reasons for wanting to watch them. In your discussion you could include such questions as:

- Why do you want to watch this program?
- What do you think you'll get out of it?
- Are you willing to forgo other activities that you really like for this program? Why?
- Of these two or three programs, which one will you choose? Why?

At this time, parents can also determine which shows will be for family viewing and which ones will be for adults only.

Talk as You Watch: Keep Basic Questions Handy

The heart of media literacy lies in the power of discussion. A free exchange of ideas gives children invaluable skills in the art of communication and provides numerous opportunities to try out ideas in a safe environment. Consistent family discussion sessions once or twice a week can have a profound effect on a child's relationship with all visual media. Through these family interactions, children gain specific knowledge that will help them throughout their lives to discern and question media messages and values. Although there is a myriad of media literacy activities that we, as parents, can participate in with our children, the most effective is talking with them about what they watch.

Managing a Family Media Literacy Discussion When your family discusses TV and video, try to cover two general areas:

- *Draw out children's own ideas about what they see on the screen.* This focuses children's attention on what is actually on the screen and helps us understand how children perceive what they view.
- *Guide children to critically examine and evaluate what they see.* Ask questions that require children to think on higher levels.

Opposite is a discussion guide that contains five sample questions for each of these two parts.

Sample Television Discussion Guide

Questions to draw out your child's ideas about screen images:

- ❑ What do you like (or dislike) about this program? Why?
- ❑ Which character/s seem the most real to you?
- ❑ What is the difference between a program and a commercial?
- ❑ Has something you've just seen scared you? made you feel uncomfortable with yourself? made you want something?
- ❑ What did you learn from this program (or movie)?

Questions to help your child think on higher levels:

- ❑ Do you think you should act the way children (or teens) act on that program? Why or why not?
- ❑ If you were writing the script, what would you make different? Why?
- ❑ When you talk to your friends about this program (or movie), what will you say? Will you mention any of the ideas we discussed? Why or why not?
- ❑ How were problems solved in the program (or movie) we just watched? Was this realistic? Why or why not? How would you have solved the problem?
- ❑ Do you think adults behave in real life the way they do on TV? Why or why not?

The following is a discussion a family became engaged in when they began addressing media literacy. The family members include: Mom, Dad, Peter (aged ten), and Susan (aged eight). This discussion took place after the family had watched *Beauty and the Beast* together on videotape.

Mom: So, what were your favorite parts?

Susan: I liked when Beauty was dancing with the Beast and when he changed into a prince!

Peter: I thought that when that mean guy fell was awesome!

Dad: I liked a lot of different parts—I'm not sure which one I liked best. The animation was classic Disney. Very good. What about you? What did you like?

Mom: I think my favorite was when they married and cleaned up that castle and had such a grand party. I liked it because it was a hopeful scene after all the sadness. The castle looked good and they looked happy.

Peter: Yeah. I wonder how the Beast could live in such a messy place.

Dad: Do you think he might have had other things on his mind other than housework?

Peter: Oh, I guess. Probably.

Mom: Like what?

Peter: Oh, he was probably feeling bad because of the magic spell.

Susan: You would too if you looked like that. You're ugly, but not that ugly! Ha ha!

Dad: Susan, that's uncalled for. Did anything upset you, even just a little, when you were watching?

Susan: Well . . . [she thinks] When they were in the dark woods. That part was scary.

Dad: Yes, it was. You know the story wasn't real, don't you, Susan?

Susan: Oh yes. But it could be.

Dad: How so?

Susan: There could be a girl who leaves her house to live with—

Peter: [interrupting] What are you saying? Of course there couldn't be a man who was changed into a beast by a witch.

Susan: Well, maybe . . . A long, long time ago.

Peter: Naw. That's a fairy tale.

Mom: Well, maybe what Susan is trying to say is that the story is a fairy tale and may be based on what actually happened a long time ago. Is that what you think, Susan?

Susan: Kind of.

Mom: Do you think a story like this could really happen today?

Susan: No, it's only a fairy tale. It's not real today.

Dad: The Beast certainly had a lot of problems, didn't he? What were some of them?

Mom: He had a dirty house.

Peter: He was ugly.

Susan: He was lonely.

Dad: How did his problems get solved?

Susan: When Beauty came she loved them away.

Peter: Yuck! Disgusting!

Mom: Yes, over time Beauty came to love the Beast for who he really was, a kind and caring creature, and not for what he looked like. That broke the spell.

Peter: Yeah, but he wanted the spell broken.

Dad: That's a good point, Peter.

Susan: Daddy, can I go now? I want to get some water.

Dad: Just a minute. I have one last question for you. What did you learn from watching this movie?

Peter: That if you wait long enough, maybe somebody will change your luck.

Mom: How come, Peter?

Peter: Because the Beast waited for Beauty to come and get rid of the spell. Then his luck changed.

Susan: If you're nice to someone, they'll be nice to you.

Dad: I think that's what I learned, too. Love can change things for the better. What do you think, hon?

Mom: Well, I have to think a little longer about what the movie has taught me. But this discussion has taught me that our kids are great at sharing ideas about what they watch.

Although these parents had attended an evening workshop on media literacy, they hadn't read any books about it, nor were they following a prescribed set of questions. For the most part, they were asking questions spontaneously, seeking information in the same manner they would ask the kids questions about the school day or an afternoon at a friend's house. In this type of relaxed discussion the children are free to express themselves without worrying about coming up with the "right answers." It doesn't really matter what sorts of questions you ask. The important thing is to listen to your children's ideas and guide them to think about what they're seeing on the screen.

Realistically, most media literacy discussions with teens will look very different from the one above. More often the talks will be spontaneous rather than planned, and they may not seem immediately successful. One father tells a story that most parents of teens might find familiar:

> I had come home from work a little earlier than usual; my wife wasn't home yet and my thirteen-year-old daughter was curled up in front of the TV supposedly doing her math homework. I started watching and soon grew livid. She was watching MTV, and the images, along with the lyrics, were shocking. I went to the TV to shut it off and my daughter said, "What do you think you're doing?" I said, "I'm turning off this garbage." She surprised me by saying, "Yeah, I can have sex ed at school but I can't watch MTV." Before she could storm out of the room I told her to wait a minute, let's look at this together and talk. Her reaction reminded me that she's not a little girl anymore, and as much as I'd like to, I can't wish away MTV. She reluctantly agreed to sit for a few minutes. Before too long another music video came on which showed women as nothing more than sex objects. As I told my daughter my thoughts about this video, she counteracted with statements like, "Don't you think I know that?" and "I don't think that's cool either." She said, "Most of the time I like the music more than the music video."
>
> I was happy to see that she was thinking about what she was watching. But since that conversation, I've made it a point to talk more about MTV and the music she brings home. Now she'll occasionally ask me to listen to a new CD and give her my opinion about it. And believe me, I do!

Talking with teens about the media may be a bit prickly at times and may require an extra dose of parental patience. Below are some reminders that may be useful when helping young adults become media literate.

Give your teen credit. Most kids do think about the messages the media send. Approach a discussion with the assumption that your child has the intellectual abilities to think through ideas and to apply valid and worthy media literacy skills.

Be open to learning something yourself. Remember when the lyrics to "Let's Spend the Night Together" shocked parents in the sixties? It's important to remain calm and open-minded, however explicit teen movies and music lyrics may be. If you discuss sensitive topics with the notion that you may learn something, your child will come to trust you and your opinions more. One parent we know was repelled by the rap lyrics her son was listening to. But with unaccustomed candidness, she approached her son to talk about her concerns. Soon, at his suggestion, she found herself reading his current favorite book, *The Ice Opinion* by the rapper Ice-T. She was so taken by it that she recommended it to her friends, explaining that she had learned so much about her son and other teens by reading the book.

Don't expect immediate results. Your teen may walk away from a family media literacy discussion sulking, but don't let that deter you. Stay cheerfully committed to keeping the lines of communication open. It may take a week or a month for your son or daughter to express an idea or opinion about a media topic. That's O.K. Be patient and give some space for your teen to sort out ideas for himself or herself. If media literacy is a family priority, your teen will eventually want to join in.

Seize the moment. If your child makes a statement about a film he wants to see, ask why and hold a discussion *before* viewing. If your child has just watched a TV program and labeled it as dumb, put down what you're doing for five minutes and investigate the reasons for that verdict. The incidental opportunities that crop up daily may be used to start enlightening discussions.

Use humor whenever possible. Exaggerating a point to the absurd is great fun, and young teens become animated when listening to satire or tall tales. "So, if you watch that action adventure film you'll want to scale the Grand Canyon, you'll think you're so invincible." Unconventional statements such as this, said in jest and with a twinkle in the eye, without putdowns, might open the door for a more serious discussion. In the case of this example, after your child groans "Oh, Mom," you could discuss the ways that stuntpeople, props, and special effects are used to create the pseudo-invincibility of heroes in action adventure films.

Helpful Pointers for Family Media Literacy Discussions Some parents find discussion guidelines helpful. You may want to try some of the suggestions below and see how they work for your family:

- *Allow your child time to think after you ask a question.* A quick response may not be possible. If you grow anxious while your child is thinking, count to ten slowly.
- *Ask questions that interest you.* Research has found that class discussions are more effective when the teachers are interested in the questions they ask and are curious about the answer. Use questions that stimulate your thinking as well as your child's.
- *Use open-ended questions as often as possible.* Questions that do not have one single answer are more effective for spurring children's higher-level thinking than questions requiring a simple yes or no.
- *If your child doesn't want to answer a question or doesn't know the answer, model an answer for him.* If you've given sufficient time for your child to reflect and he still isn't coming up with anything, move on to another family member or gently tell him what you think. Avoid pressuring. You can say something like, "If you come up with an idea later, I'd love to know what you think." If you consistently probe without pressuring, over time the youngster will learn to participate more fully in family discussions.

Encourage the Three C's — Communication, Critical Thinking, and Creativity

The process of becoming media literate requires the need to develop and practice good communication skills, critical thinking abilities, and a creative approach to content.

Communication It's apparent that communication skills and critical thinking skills are practiced during family discussions about TV programs or movies. But what may come as a surprise is that the more you talk with children about the visual media, the more *they* want to talk with you about them. You might find your shy seven-year-old suddenly volunteering information at the dinner table about a video she saw in school, or your ten-year-old revealing his ideas about a video game he played at a friend's house. Once children learn the basic principles of analyzing visual images, they'll start doing it naturally and initiate media literacy discussions more often. One mother who had been working on media literacy for six months describes an experience with her fourteen-year-old son:

> It was the end of summer and we were eating dinner at a little outdoor café, taking a break from shopping for school clothes. My son, Mark, pointed out to me that the people at the table next to us had three movies: *Poltergeist 3, Friday the 13th,* and *Nightmare on Elm Street.* He nudged me and said, "Mom, I think these people need some media literacy. They're going to show those movies to their little kids." I couldn't have been more pleased that he was that observant! From there we talked about a variety of things: possible age and education requirements for children to see such films, if such films were even worth viewing, and what kind of horror flicks he'd like to see. It was great. When we eat out, he usually doesn't talk much. But he had a lot to say this time.

Critical Thinking When parents pose intellectually challenging questions during family media literacy discussions, the conversation grows more sophisticated. Educators have long recognized that asking children intelligent questions is made easier when critical thinking skills are broken down into different types. Listed below are seven types of thinking skills, along with sample questions that parents can use in discussions:

- *Details*—What time of year did the story take place? Can you describe the scenery? the clothes the characters wore? Who wore glasses?
- *Sequence*—Relate the events of the plot in the order they happened. What were the main events in the movie?
- *Prediction of outcome*—What might happen next? How could the movie have ended differently? Since you saw the first program in this television series, what do you think the next one will be about?
- *Cause and effect*—Who was responsible for major events in the program? How was the conflict resolved? What caused the conflict?

- *Inference*—Why does the character make certain decisions? How do you think the writers arrived at this story idea? What do the characters' actions say about their personalities?
- *Context clues*—Judging by the title, what do you think this program will be about? When you look at the packaging of this video, what do you think the subject matter will be? Since this character always acts in a certain manner, how will this person (or another character on the program) react to him?
- *Symbolic thinking*—Why did Coke use polar bears in their commercials? Why not tigers or elephants? What is the significance of the women being put into cages in this video? What if the men were in cages instead?

Creativity Creativity is sometimes thought of as a special gift that some of us are given. Not so. We are all being creative when we produce something that is original to us. For instance, when we adapt a recipe because we're out of the listed ingredients and we come up with a delicious meal, we are being creative. When we find a way to juggle a full schedule of household tasks, family obligations, social responsibilities, career, and children, we are certainly being creative. Creativity is a natural human trait, and we call upon it daily, not only to design something new, but to solve the problems that always crop up in life.

When teaching media literacy, it can be fun to exercise children's creativity muscles. This is a time to pull out all stops, to mix it up, to think far-out and far-fetched. As the educator Edward deBono points out: "Creativity involves breaking out of established patterns in order to look at things in a different way."[9] Let the creative ideas bubble up and put the media in an entirely different light. This approach teaches our children to think in innovative ways and beckons us to look at screen images as things to explore from a carefree, lighthearted perspective.

There are many activities in this book that spur creativity. But don't limit yourself to these. Remember that creative thinking is possibility thinking. Give your child's and your own imagination free rein and see what happens.

Creative Possibilities

What would happen if…

- You and the kids watched a favorite show as if you were important critics and discussed it afterwards in character…
- You put a sheet over the TV and said nothing when the kids came home from school…
- You pretended to be a parent from one of your child's favorite sitcoms and acted just like that parent all through dinner one evening…
- You rented an educational video about some natural setting, such as the Olympic rain forests or Yellowstone National Park, and you planned a family picnic in front of it, complete with picnic basket…
- You turned off the sound and each person watching became a character and made up the dialogue as the show went along…
- You spent one night a week drawing on your home screens with washable, colored markers…
- You communicated to family members what happened in your favorite show without using words and invited others to do the same…
- You invited neighbors and friends over for dessert and a discussion about the latest popular movie…

Media Literacy and Cyberspace

It is difficult to grasp the fact that screen technologies are still in their infancy. The twenty-first century will witness an explosion of ever-more-sophisticated cyberspace highways which will become integral to every aspect of our children's lives. This does not necessarily mean, however, that all the information gained will be used wisely or appropriately. Nor does it mean that the information is worth having. Indeed, the word *shovelware* has been coined to define redundant and useless information available on-line. Although computer systems, information networks, and virtual reality hold great promise, they pose some parental challenges as well.

Computer Software and Multimedia

From looking up a word in a dictionary to learning an Indonesian folk song to designing your own house, computer software is available for an amazingly wide variety of purposes. Programs that were unaffordable only a few years ago are now well within our price range. And as the technology advances, people are incorporating it more and more into their daily lives. For instance, laptops aren't just for businesspeople anymore—families are taking them on vacations as a convenient way to keep a journal of vacation highlights and to monitor expenses. Distant relatives keep in touch with one another via computer-generated newsletters and modems. And it has become commonplace, even required, for children to turn in polished homework assignments prepared on a computer.

No matter the age, all children benefit greatly from computer programs that allow them to manipulate ideas, explore new concepts, and create tangible products. Many parents are delighted when they see their little ones interacting with a computer, and well they should be. Computer software that engages children's creativity can help them learn and think in new ways.

Software that provides a wide range of possible outcomes, rather than one right or wrong answer, bolsters a child's confidence. School-age children benefit greatly when educational software reinforces skills learned in school. Older children and adolescents also gain advantages from computer software. With success, their self-esteem blossoms. And the more often your child derives a sense of pride from his accomplishments, the more he will strive to learn.

Dr. Jane Healy, an authority on child development in a media age, states, "Making children into 'watchers,' or program manipulators, as opposed to 'originators' is an alarming perversion of childhood's developmental tasks."[10] When children are encouraged to come up with original ideas when playing computer games, they are required to think on sophisticated levels. This type of practice at home relates to school success. Parents can support their children in this effort by sitting with the child as s/he plays the game and by asking questions: "What are your ideas about how this game works?" "If you were developing this computer software, what would you do differently?" "What do you like best (or least) about this game?" "You've been playing for an hour now; show me what you've learned."

Just as media-literate children learn to schedule time watching television, so too can they learn to limit and schedule time on the computer. It will help if time working at the computer is planned ahead, so that children learn to balance it with other activities. Helen, the mother of a preschooler, shares her experience:

> I used to defend my four-year-old's habit of spending three hours a day playing computer games. "At least she's playing *Reader Rabbit* and other educational games rather than violent games," I rationalized. Jenny is quite precocious and is learning a good deal from these games. But after attending a workshop on media literacy, I realized that Jenny is in front of a screen instead of playing with her toys for a good fifteen hours a week. If young kids need a lot of activity and tactile experiences in order to learn best, I'm not doing Jenny a favor by not limiting computer time along with TV time.

Information Networks

Neighborhood by neighborhood, every home in the United States will eventually have the ability to receive and send information about any subject anywhere in the world. The amount of information that is exchanged on a single computer network is mind-boggling. One observer estimates: "Probably more words are put out in a week by the 20 million people who use the loosely strung computer networks that constitute the Internet than are published by all major American publishing companies in a year."[11]

While adults make up the majority of drivers on these information highways, older children and teens are rapidly discovering it. It may be tempting to keep these information systems off-limits to our kids because of the distasteful, and even dangerous, information they carry. But in this media age, there are always risks: risks of a five-year-old encountering a slasher film on cable; risks of a thirteen-year-old having access to an R-rated movie; risks of reading the wrong book at the library. However, emphasis must be placed on the benefits of discovering new interests rather than on the dangers that lurk behind those bulletin boards. Parents who are computer literate feel more comfortable helping their children to navigate potential dangers. The steps below prepare children and teens for the journeys they will take on the complex information highway.

- *Set boundaries.* Make sure your child is absolutely clear on what territory he is free to roam and what is off-limits. Restrict modem access to what is in accordance with your family's values. You may want to purchase the software that limits children's access, giving you peace of mind.
- *Set time limits.* Corresponding by E-mail with a pen pal in Europe may be educational and great fun, but make sure screen life doesn't dominate.
- *Direct learning.* Encourage your child to learn as much as possible about the system's advantages, drawbacks, and limitations. S/he can take a course or read a book to glean important information.
- *Encourage exploration.* When on a system such as the Internet, encourage your child to ask questions and answer them by trial and error, experimenting with the system's options. Nurture the excitement and joy of discovery.
- *Promote new interests.* Ask questions that promote new interests. For instance, if you think your child might be interested in the game of chess, ask, "Where can you find bulletin boards that advertise for chess-playing partners?" If he's studying the Civil War in school, you might ask, "Can you locate a book that would help you with your school report on the Civil War?"

Virtual Reality

Immersive environments, as they are sometimes called, offer the most exciting interactive electronic formats currently available. In the HIV/AIDS virtual reality game, designed by at-risk high school students, the user is in "an immune-system cell navigating through a world in which HIV cells float menacingly in the air. Also floating in the air are objects representing infection-prevention strategies:

Criteria for Choosing Computer Software for Your Child

- *Age appropriateness*—Is your child the right age for this software? You may have to preview the program or game to determine this. Does it contain vocabulary or concepts your child won't understand?
- *Content*—Does it teach or entertain? What does it teach? Is it something your child needs to learn? Will it challenge your child without frustrating him?
- *Technical merit*—Are the graphics clear and effective? Can your child read the text? Are the graphics and sounds related to what's being taught? Are they sophisticated enough to keep your child's interest but not so sophisticated that he'll find them boring?
- *Values*—How does the program or game portray women? minorities? the elderly? Does it reflect values that you support? How might the content of this software affect your child's attitudes and behaviors?
- *Long-term education*—Does this software allow your child to keep track of what she's learned, so that she has a record of her progress? Do skills progressively become more challenging, building upon one another? Will the software sustain your child's interest?
- *Types of thinking*—Does this program offer intellectual stimulation? Are there plenty of open-ended questions? Is there little emphasis on simple yes and no answers and more emphasis on thinking?
- *Personal involvement*—Does the program offer your child plenty of opportunities to be innovative and inventive? Will your child's originality be incorporated? Will your child see the results of his creativity?

Questions for Determining Family Media Literacy Progress

- *Frequency*—How often do we as a family use TV, video, and computers? How often are the children in front of a screen? Is this at the expense of other activities pertinent to their development? Do the children regularly choose other activities for amusement? Are their lives balanced?
- *Content*—What do we watch as a family? Are all the children's programs appropriate for their age and level of maturity? How do we make decisions about appropriate content for the family? for the children?
- *Discussion*—Do we regularly talk about what we watch? Is this an enjoyable family activity in and of itself? Are the children's responses growing more sophisticated over time? Are they evaluating TV programs, movies, and video games on their own?

bleach bottles, zipped jeans, condoms, and sterile hypodermics. The player attempts to grab as many of these objects as possible while avoiding contact with the HIV cells. The more . . . prevention objects the player can collect, the more powerfully and faster he or she can move through the virtual world."[12]

This game is a good example of new methods of education made possible by virtual reality. Virtual reality provides unlimited potential as an instructional tool and as a creative outlet—children take to this three-dimensional experience with enormous enthusiasm. The high school students who designed the HIV/AIDS game learned to run the imaging and animation software simply by experimentation. Attendance throughout the project's duration was much higher than usual because the students were strongly motivated by this new technology.

Virtual reality can be troubling for children, however, because the experience so accurately represents real life. Monitor the extent of violence and content of VR games and be certain they are appropriate for your child's age and level of maturity.

Making Media Literacy Part of Everyday Life

It is indisputable that children enjoy interacting with television, video, and computers. Academic research as well as parents' observations alert us to the fact that the earlier children learn to discuss visual messages, the better. We know that the cumulative effects of a passive television habit are detrimental to our children and that the cumulative effects of family media literacy are astoundingly beneficial. Armed with media literacy skills, children and teenagers will reflect upon visual technology's role in their lives; they will understand its power, analyze its messages, and learn to use it wisely.

3

Bam! Smash! Pow! Screen Violence

Guns, knives, ropes, machetes, steel fists . . . by the age of twelve, children in the United States have witnessed approximately 20,000 murders and 80,000 assaults on television.[1] That is an extraordinary number of horrific images to be taken in at a time when emotional maturity and social behaviors are evolving.

In television's infancy, broadcasting pioneers promised that the new technology would bring the best of everything—science, history, music, the arts, drama. They described TV as "the university of the air."[2] Each network even had its own studio orchestra offering classical music as background to such thoughtful adult programs as Edward R. Murrow's *See It Now.* Many, many children's shows were offered. Programs such as *Kukla, Fran and Ollie, Howdy Doody, Captain Kangaroo, Mr. Wizard,* and *Captain Video* shared the innocence and joy of the child's world, delighting as well as educating them. In fact, by 1955 there were more shows for children than there were soap operas, variety, news or dramatic shows.[3] The purpose of television was to uplift and inspire, as well as to entertain. This golden age of television lasted for only a few years. It soon became apparent that these programs, however noble in their intent, were not attracting the larger viewing audience. Advertisers wanted higher numbers. But how to get them?

As more and more families bought TV sets, mostly at the insistence of the children, they soon became affordable to the average middle-class family, and a mass audience was born. To draw this large population, producers began to program to what they called the lowest common denominator.[4] Westerns such as *Gunsmoke* and crime dramas such as *The Untouchables* dominated prime time. These violent, action-packed shows immediately captivated adult viewers. By the late fifties cultural programming had mostly faded, for producers had discovered the key to television's future: fast-paced, shoot-'em-up programs.[5]

Violent Images: What's the Big Deal?

Today, from the larger than life movie screens to the tiniest pocket Game Boy, children have a constant stream of violent images readily available to them. Why do we offer violence as the mainstay of their amusement? Why is it that a human maiming and killing another human is considered appropriate entertainment for children?

Part of the lure of violent images, many experts believe, is that they arouse our basic instinct for survival. A fast-moving story plot or video game with a constant stream of violence keeps the adrenaline pumping and the reptilian brain on alert. If the brain is preoccupied with potential danger, the cerebral cortex is hard-pressed to think coherently. In effect, violent images arouse *instincts and feelings* while restraining the *reasoning* functions.

And, the more violent the action, the more likely children are to keep watching. This is because every violent action requires a change of image—that is, a very quick scene change. Continual scene changes arouse the primitive instinct to look at what might be dangerous. Experts call this the orienting response. Our reptilian and limbic brain systems urge us to look at sudden changes in our environment. The greater number of scene changes, then, the greater our propensity to continue watching. In fact, many of today's prominent television experts believe that the actual change of image is what holds TV viewers' attention—not the content, sound, color, or quality of acting.[6]

The images in children's cartoons change on average every three to five seconds, and their violence levels are higher than those in any type of adult programming. In one study, 2,000 violent scenes were observed in 180 hours of programming.[7] MTV's music videos convey an image change every second or less and contain twice the amount of violence found in prime-time programming.[8]

Never before has the theme of graphic and gratuitous violence so overwhelmed screen content. We're not saying that exemplary TV programs, movies, and video games aren't available to children—they are. What we are saying is that as children watch thousands of violent acts or play intense video games, their attention is taken away from the consequences of real human suffering. These images serve to distort ideas about pain and death. And, in the case of video games, violent images are connected with feelings of exhilaration, accomplishment, and conquest. They offer not a means of coming to terms with violence and human nature but a reinforcement of violence as a way of life.

Creating the Need for Violence

When children watch numerous traumatic shows on television and spend a good deal of time playing violent video games, they may come to require increasingly horrific programming to feel an emotional response. And, in time, even the most violent of screen images will have less of an effect, possibly leading one to seek violent "thrills" in the real world.[9]

This cycle of "stimulus addiction," as it is sometimes called, may be easily started when young children, exposed to media violence, develop a psychological and biological need for increasingly violent entertainment. Paul Gathercoal, an expert on media studies in Australia, explains: "Constant and prolonged exposure to screen violence can affect us in two ways: We may actually physically need our daily 'fix' of violent programming, and we can build up an immunity to horrific media images and become incapable of producing socially acceptable emotional responses."[10]

On the other hand, if children are exposed to a greater variety of slower-moving, thoughtful images, they are likely to see manufactured violence for what it is. In contrast to violent programs, movies, and video games, which don't allow much time for critical thinking,

Cycle Effects from Long-Term Viewing of Television Violence

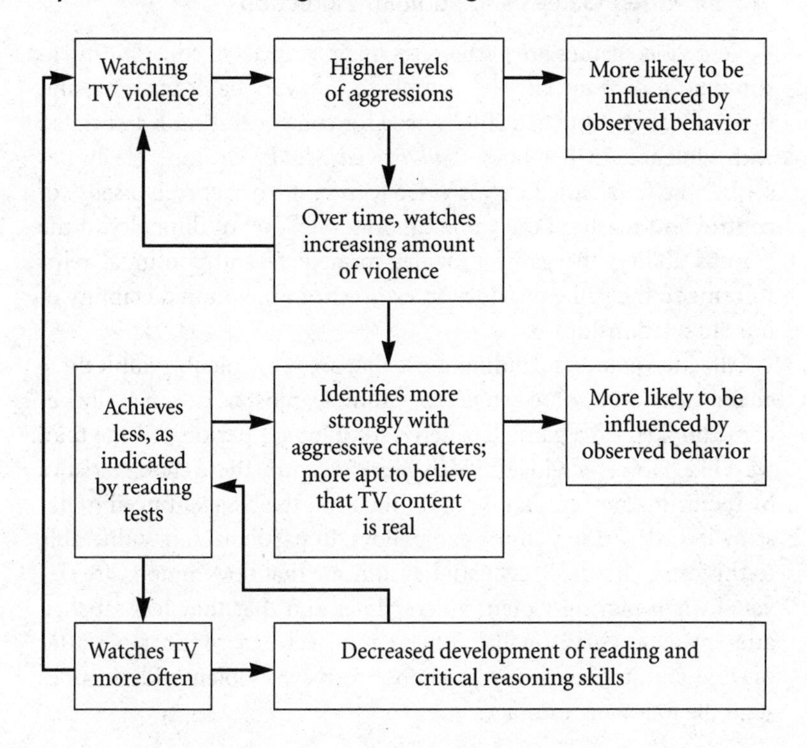

quality programs keep the child mentally alert and physiologically calm. Because slower-moving screen images require conscious thinking processes by the intensive engagement of the cerebral cortex, they tend to be analyzed and evaluated in ways that violent programs aren't.

When a five-year-old watches a program such as *Mr. Rogers,* for instance, she has to expend effort to concentrate on what he is saying. Mr. Rogers moves and talks slowly—much like people do in the real world—in order to give the child time to process what is being said or shown. When that same child watches fast-paced cartoons, which often carry more than twenty-four violent acts per hour, she barely uses her own powers of concentration.[11]

Violent Video Games and Stimulus Addiction

Violent video games are perhaps the main culprits in contributing to stimulus addiction. They are simple to use, very habit forming, and they may contribute to a child's need for continual stimuli associated with violence. In her book *Endangered Minds,* Dr. Jane Healy describes the four basic lures of video games: the player feels a sense of control and mastery; the game calibrates its level of difficulty to the player's ability; the game provides immediate and continual reinforcement; the game provides an escape from the unpredictability of human relationships.[12]

All video games, including those that are nonviolent, exhibit these characteristics to some extent. For example, most of us can easily become hooked on a game like Tetris for a longer period of time than we'd like. However, violent video games magnify these characteristics by requiring our reptilian brain to focus on the constant need to destroy in order to stay in the game. Boys, in particular, are vulnerable to this call to battle. Recent studies indicate that boys' moods are elevated when playing violent video games and that they feel satisfied after playing. Girls, on the other hand, feel less comfortable after playing and are less likely to choose to play.[13] Violent video games send the following messages:

- Problems can be resolved quickly and with little personal investment.
- The best way to solve a problem is to eliminate the source of the problem.
- Look at problems in terms of black and white, right or wrong.
- Use instinctual behaviors to react to problems, not thoughtful, responsible behavior.
- Personal imagination is not an important problem-solving skill.
- It is acceptable to immerse oneself in the video game's rule-driven reality without questioning the rules.

Contrast the above with what children learn when they play maze games, puzzles, and simulation or treasure hunt video games:

- Problems are solved through patience, personal initiative, perseverance, tolerance, and flexibility.
- Gathering information requires work, and information must be carefully analyzed in order to be of help when making informed decisions.
- Defining and solving problems involves using complex skills.
- A solution in one instance might not work as a solution in another instance.
- It is important to use critical and creative thinking skills such as planning actions, organizing information, predicting outcomes, experimenting with trial solutions, evaluating ideas, and analyzing solutions and their consequences.
- Use personally generated, thoughtful responses to solve problems.
- Use imagination and thinking abilities to co-create, with the game's writer, inventive situations.

These types of games not only develop children's imaginative abilities but also expand their view of the world, offering alternatives to the distorted world of violent video games. As Eugene Provenzo observes in his book *Video Kids,* "[Violent] video games ... are neither neutral nor harmless, but represent very specific social and symbolic constructs. In effect, the games become powerful teaching machines and instruments of cultural transmission."[14]

The Experts Voice Their Concern about Media Violence

Hundreds of research studies worldwide have been conducted on media violence and its relationship to real-life violence. It would be ludicrous to proclaim that screen violence is the only cause of violent behavior. It isn't. However, a large body of evidence indicates that screen violence is a significant contributing factor to violent behavior, especially when the habit of viewing violence is started early in childhood.

Experts who have been researching the issue are voicing their concern. The following contributions were made from 1976 through 1994:

A Sampling of Nonviolent Video Games

For Young Children
Mario Paint, Nintendo of America
Mario's Early Years: Pre-School Fun, Mindscape
Math Blaster, Davidson Associates
Thomas the Tank Engine and Friends, THQ

For Older Children and Teens
Where in Time Is Carmen Sandiego?, Hi-Tech Entertainment
The Brainies, Titus Software
Tetris 2, Nintendo of America
Monopoly, Parker Brothers
NBA Live '95, Hitmen Productions

1976—The House of Delegates of the American Medical Association passes a resolution, after deliberating on the evidence, that TV violence contributes to real-life violence. They issue the following statement: "Resolved, that the American Medical Association: 1. Declares its recognition of the fact that TV violence is a risk factor threatening the health and welfare of young Americans, indeed our future society. 2. Commits itself to remedial action in concert with industry, government, and other interested parties. 3. Encourages all physicians, their families, and their patients to actively oppose TV programs containing violence, as well as products and/or services sponsoring such programs."[15]

1982—The National Institute of Mental Health reviews 2,500 worldwide studies on the effects of media violence and concludes that there is a great deal of evidence to suggest a link between watching violence and becoming more violent.[16]

1984—Professors Leonard Eron and L. Rowell Huesman release their findings of a 22-year study in which they followed the same group of 875 boys and girls from ages 8 to 30. They find that those who watched more violent television as children were more likely as adults to commit serious crimes and to use violence to punish their own children. Professor Eron concludes, "What one learns about life from the television screen seems to be transmitted to the next generation."[17]

1992—The American Psychological Association issues the report *Big World, Small Screen.* The nine distinguished contributors state that TV violence is "strongly correlated with aggressive behavior ... the research question has moved from asking whether or not there is an effect to seeking explanations for the effect."[18]

1993—A conference is held, sponsored by the Department of Justice, the Department of Education, and the Department of Health and Human Services, entitled "Safeguarding Our Youth: Violence Prevention for Our Nation's Children." Experts agree that the social effects of media violence must be considered in any programs that are designed to address the problems of youth violence and that "broad-based media literacy education needs to become a priority in the U.S. and implemented in an interagency, interdisciplinary approach."[19]

1994—The Center for Media and Public Affairs conducts a study of television violence and finds that from 1992 to 1994, depictions of serious violence on television increased 67 percent, violence in promos almost doubled, and violence in network and local news programs increased 244 percent.[20]

Media Violence and Child Development

Researchers have identified four basic effects of exposure to screen violence. While these apply to adults as well as children, children are the most vulnerable to them:

- *Increased aggression and hostility*—Children who are exposed to media violence on a regular basis will be more likely to exhibit a hostile attitude, more reactionary and defensive in social interactions, more likely to resolve conflicts with physical force, and more likely to use bullying behaviors as an overall approach to life.
- *Increased fear*—Night terrors, overconcern for self-protection,

fear of being alone, and untrusting behaviors are symptoms associated with those who watch a good deal of violence.

- *Increased callousness and insensitivity*—Continuous exposure to manufactured horror makes a person less empathetic to real-life suffering, less caring to those who are hurting, and less capable of responding appropriately to those in need.
- *Increased appetite for violence*—The more violence a person watches, the more they wish to see, especially if the habit is formed in early childhood.[21]

These effects are more likely to set in when children watch violent images without the benefit of adult guidance. Child development specialists outline three important considerations regarding how children react to screen violence:

- Children unwittingly imitate what they see
- Children need help from adults to understand cause and effect
- The habit of watching media violence, if started early, may last a lifetime

Children Unwittingly Imitate What They See

A kindergarten teacher relates the following incident:

> One of the most distressing things I saw recently was a situation in which five boys were playing together, taking one another "hostage" by grabbing the hostage around the neck from behind and placing their hands, shaped as pistols, up to his head. They were yelling and walking him backwards. Then the child holding him pretended to shoot the victim in the temple, then released him. The others then put the "shooter" on his knees, said a few words, and pretended to shoot him in the back of the head. He fell forward and the others ran away. When I spoke with them about the "game," they informed me that they "see that kind of stuff on TV all the time." They said, "That's what you do to bad guys."

A teacher and mother of four-year-old and one-year-old girls relates this incident:

> We had just finished watching the TV program *Batman.* I put the girls in the bathtub and I was about to go into the hall for some towels when I saw my four-year-old holding her sister's head down under the water. I raced to the baby and had to shake her a bit to get the water out of her airway. I was terrified. And I felt very lucky to have been near enough to prevent a tragedy. It wasn't until a few hours later that I suddenly realized my four-year-old was imitating Batman's behavior —right before bathtime she had watched him hold an enemy underwater until he drowned him.

Children do imitate what they see. This is Mother Nature's way of ensuring that they learn adult behaviors. Dr. Brandon Centerwall, who has spent more than twenty years studying the effects of media violence, states: "Whereas infants (and young children) have an instinctual desire to imitate observed human behavior, they do not possess an instinct for gauging whether a behavior ought to be imitated. They will imitate anything, including behaviors most adults would regard as destructive and antisocial. It may give pause for thought, then, to learn that infants as young as fourteen months of age demonstrably observe and incorporate behaviors seen on television."[22] Studies have found that 22 to 34 percent of young male felons imprisoned for violent crimes such as homicide, rape, and assault reported having consciously imitated crime techniques learned from TV programs.[23] Most children's screen imitation results in somewhat milder, though still disturbing, behavior. Shoving, kicking, and punching siblings and friends are behaviors most often reported by parents, teachers, and researchers.

Since 1982, television violence has increased 780 percent. In this same time period, elementary teachers have reported a nearly 800 percent increase in aggressive acts on the playground.[24] Some schools have canceled outdoor recess entirely. Many others are implementing curricula that teach children cooperative techniques and peaceful conflict resolution. The need for such intervention increases as our children's problems with hostility and aggression increase.

Left alone, children are not always mature enough to react appropriately to what they see on the screen. They often cannot analyze events or make the distinction between reality and fantasy, and they often mimic what they see without fully understanding that they're doing so. They adopt the attitudes portrayed on the screen as their own, unaware of where those attitudes come from. They need guidance from caring adults to understand that what they see on television and in the movies is not real.

Understanding Cause and Effect

Young children are particularly influenced by screen violence. Brain research suggests that this is because most children younger than the age of eight or nine have immature analytical abilities. Young children do not have the capability to make good sense of violent behavior on the screen—they operate in an experiential world where firsthand experiences are readily understandable, yet events removed from their direct experiences are much more difficult to grasp. The screen introduces a level of abstraction that moves the behavior outside the realm of concrete, direct experience.

The fantasy world of TV can also seduce older children and teens into forgetting about real-life consequences. All too often we read about a teen whose reaction to a real shooting is, "It never looked this bloody on TV." Kids can disconnect an act of violence on the screen from genuine human pain and apply a callousness to actual events. In fact, adolescent development specialists are alarmed by the increasing insensitivity of many of our youth, and they point to media violence as one significant reason for this. Teenagers, because they have more advanced critical reasoning abilities than young children do, can benefit a great deal from understanding the effects of violence in the media.

A Media Violence Habit Can Last a Lifetime

A child's mind is like wet cement—impressionable. Activities that reoccur frequently in childhood tend to have an imprinting effect: That is, they become part of the child's personality. If the mind is continually etched with the same information, it becomes grooved and eventually hardens into that groove, creating a habit. Parents know how this works. Kids can be conditioned to pick up their rooms, brush their teeth regularly, and do household chores. But it takes constant repetition and consistent encouragement until the behaviors become so internalized that the child performs the tasks without parental prodding.

Because the child's brain is malleable, it is susceptible to *negative* conditioning. A habit that is detrimental to a child's growth is formed in the same way a healthy habit is formed. If a child sees violent acts day in and day out, his brain becomes conditioned to rely on them in order to feel satisfied. The viewing of violent images can become a daily habit that is very difficult to break.

A habit of watching screen violence affects not only children's social development but their mental development as well. Researchers have found that there are feedback loops that, over time, create vicious cycle effects from long-term exposure to screen violence. In general, the more a child watches TV, the more she watches violence, the less she reads, and the less able she is to develop her critical thinking skills. This, in turn, leads to more viewing and less thinking. The poorer the child's academic achievement and the greater her inclination toward aggressive behavior, the more she is susceptible to the cumulative effects of these feedback loops.[25] (See diagram on page 57.)

It's O.K. for Parents to Say No

Setting appropriate boundaries and restrictions on what we deem inappropriate is one of the most challenging parental tasks in today's video world. Yet protecting our children from violent images will pay huge dividends as they mature. Backed by information from the cumulative research, parents can feel entirely justified in believing that a no answer is the best thing for their child. The following suggestions may help parents enforce limits:

Provide a distraction. Young children in particular will forget about an unfulfilled request for screen viewing when an enticing alternative is provided: a new coloring book, a jaunt in the park, cookie baking, or special time with a parent, friend, relative, or sibling. Sometimes even older children surprise us with how easily they can be distracted. One mother, Betty, used distraction to lure her kids from a Friday night TV show she thought inappropriate:

After school on Friday, Betty announced that the family was going bowling that evening. Her ten-year-old son and twelve-year-old daughter, enthused at the prospect, asked her to videotape "their" show so that they wouldn't miss it. Betty agreed and did so. The next Friday the family went bowling again, only this time Betty conveniently "forgot" to tape the program for the kids. They were disappointed, but no major hassle ensued. By the third week, the kids forgot to ask to tape the program. By the fourth week, Betty's family decided that Friday evening was "family night"—a night reserved for special plans. Betty couldn't afford to take them out every Friday, so she and the kids made a list of fun at-home activities like playing charades and other games, making meals from a variety of ethnic cuisines, and doing art projects, along with a list of inexpensive outings like a trip to the local library followed by an ice cream sundae. After several months, the kids finally realized that they were "missing" their show. Betty then told them she thought it was inappropriate and why. "Besides, aren't we having more fun now on Friday evenings?" To her amazement they listened to her explanations about the show, didn't raise any objections, and agreed with her!

Say "No, for now." It helps for a child to have hope. Doug's nine-year-old son had been pestering him for days to see a movie that Doug felt was inappropriate. A parental "No" wasn't working. Doug explained that the movie was too violent, that it was banned in other parts of the world for children under twelve, and that it just wasn't right for a nine-year-old kid. But his explanations fell flat. All his son's friends had seen it. So Doug used the metaphor of a hot stove and gave his son some hope: "Remember when you were little and we didn't let you near the stove?" he reminded his son. "You could have easily burned yourself because you were too little to know its potential danger. Now that you're older you can use the stove without getting hurt. This movie is like the hot stove. Right now you're too young to understand its potential dangers. When you're older, say fourteen or fifteen, we'll watch the movie together and talk about it. How about it?" His son slowly accepted the explanation—it made sense to him and gave him something to look forward to.

Join forces with other parents. Saying no can be that much easier when parents have the support of other adults. Befriending the parents of our kids' chums can be an efficient measure in the effort to protect them from screen violence. After all, your child's friends are very influential. Engaging in thoughtful discussions with other concerned parents can result in effective problem solving. Joining forces creates a united front for the children involved and helps relieve some of the peer pressure. It also helps us understand that we are not alone and that other parents are dealing with similar issues.

Is Media Violence Ever O.K. for Children?

There are two types of media violence. The first type reflects the human condition and the horrors of suffering, and the second glamorizes and sensationalizes cruelty and brutality. The latter is violence for violence's sake—it's the type children can do without. Children must learn to distinguish the two types of screen violence.

The following questions will help kids discern whether screen violence is sensational or sensitive. Parents should discuss these questions and keep children's attention focused on healthy portrayals of violence, on those that have learning potential.

How frequent is the violence? Is there one violent act after another? Is the plot driven by violence? The shooting of the dog in the movie *Sounder*, for instance, is a violent act: we see the dog hurt; we see him suffer and then run off; we don't learn he has survived until the end of the film. Contrast this violence with the type found in a video game such as *Mortal Kombat II*. Selective uses of violence within a realistic story context enable children to recognize the tragedy of violence.

Is the violence funny? There is nothing funny about hurting another human being. Yet much of what passes for children's entertainment these days is the inhumane treatment of others. *Home Alone II*, a movie made for kids, ran the gamut from torture techniques to sadistic revenge while its young audience laughed uproariously throughout. Experts agree that it is harmful and downright dangerous to society as a whole to classify depictions of people hurting one another as entertainment.

Is the violence portrayed as "cool"? Brutal killing machines that are untouched by human emotion and unconcerned about human suffering are not appropriate heroes for children. Often these "heroes" use violence and force twice as often as the antagonists do. When violence is made glamorous by seemingly powerful men, many children, especially boys, imitate their behavior in order to be "cool." Girls learn that they are more likely to be victims and get the message that females are powerless.

Is the violence graphic and gory? Malcolm X was a violent movie. Yet the violence shown was selective and never extremely graphic. In contrast, another film starring Denzel Washington, *Ricochet,* contained gratuitous violence such as a bloody body hanging from the ceiling and close-ups of metal spokes being forcefully driven into a person's abdomen. The portrayal was sensational, not sensitive. Many of the violent scenes were entirely unnecessary for the film's plot.

Countering Media Violence with Media Literacy

The issue of screen violence in our society is overwhelming. As parents, we at times feel helpless to protect our children and teach them realistic ways to cope with it. However, we should certainly attempt to address the issue. Listed below are some media literacy strategies that have worked for us and for many parents we know.

Keep a list of acceptable TV programs and videos handy. This "emergency list" can be priceless for the hassles it prevents. Choose titles that provide images and role models you wouldn't mind your child imitating. Engage your child in the process of making up the list. Discuss the attributes and the weaknesses of the videos your child wants to see. If you think the videos are marginal ones, make an agreement: Your child can watch them provided you watch also and s/he talks with you afterwards.

A list of preselected videos can be helpful when:

- ❑ Your child wants to have a video for her slumber party.
- ❑ Your child has been invited to spend the night with a friend. The friend provides the pizza; your child brings the video they'll be watching.

- ❑ Your child complains he can't watch anything on TV, that you're being too mean.
- ❑ Your child is home sick from school and doesn't feel well enough to do anything besides "veg out" in front of the screen.
- ❑ Your child is upset because you've said no to a particular TV show or video.
- ❑ You'd like your child to be occupied because you must get some work done around the house.

Block cable channels you don't want your children to watch. Cable companies don't make a big noise about it, but you can have certain stations blocked out. How? Contact your local cable company and make a request. Different companies offer different services. In some instances, the viewer can delete any channel she wishes if she has a converter box and a remote control. Or the viewer makes a phone call and the cable company dispatches a worker to the home to put a "trap on the line" on the telephone pole. You don't have to tolerate channels that make you uncomfortable in order to benefit from good programming.

Remind children that screen violence is not real; talk about it often. As frequently as possible, discuss the fact that screen violence is manufactured. Someone wrote the script, planned the stunts, designed the special effects, performed the stunts, took the pictures. And everyone walks away healthy and unhurt. Very far from reality.

Discuss the reasons for watching violent images. Why would anyone want to hurt anyone else in the first place? What are the consequences in real life when we inflict injury on another person? What is the purpose of watching violence? What's the reason to play a violent video game?

Encourage your children to read about real people who suffered at the hands of violence. Many children are given opportunities at school to hear lectures by people who have encountered violence. Veterans' Day assemblies often feature our country's veterans, who talk about their experiences at war. More and more schools are bringing in police officers, ex-convicts, and ex–gang members to discuss the eye-opening consequences of street violence. Listening to these types of

Recommended Videos

For children aged three to seven:
Curious George, The Mouse and the Motorcycle, Pecos Bill, Morris Goes to School, The Velveteen Rabbit, The Red Shoes, Dr. Desoto, Meet Your Animal Friends, Raffi in Concert, Hop on Pop, The Red Balloon, The Snowman.

For children aged seven to twelve:
The Electric Grandmother, Be a Juggler, Molly's Pilgrim, Bearskin, Free Willy, The Mighty Ducks, The Sandlot, Nutcracker: The Motion Picture, Tommy, The Cosmic Eye, Where the Red Fern Grows, Pistol: The Birth of a Legend, Anne of Green Gables, The Black Stallion, To Kill a Mockingbird.

For children aged twelve to fourteen:
Rudy, Heart and Souls, Flowers for Algernon, Stand and Deliver, All Creatures Great and Small, The Whales of August, Lucas, Looking for Miracles, Murphy's Romance, Necessary Parties, Never Cry Wolf, West Side Story, Breaking Away.

experiences and then discussing them helps both children and teens to appreciate the horrors of real-life violence.

One mother had success with a creative idea: Mary was tired of hearing her fifteen-year-old son, Dan, say that "violence is cool." Dan was a bright boy who thought violence was the best way to solve problems, especially problems with bullies. She decided that every time she found an article in the paper about a child or teen dying or suffering at the hand of a violent predator, she would clip it out and display it prominently on the refrigerator door. Her husband joined her in the effort, and soon they had accumulated more articles than could fit on ten refrigerator doors. Every night for a week they chose several compelling articles, read them aloud to Dan, and then discussed them with him. It wasn't long before Dan was getting the picture about the terrible consequences of real-life violence.

Choosing the Best for Our Kids

Our children deserve the best entertainment we can offer. The following lists summarize the qualities to look for in TV programs, movies, and video games. Choose ones that:

- ❑ Portray suffering and the human condition sensitively
- ❑ Evoke thoughtful family discussion
- ❑ Reflect your priorities and values
- ❑ Enhance your child's learning about herself and others

Choose video and computer games that:

- ❑ Demand mental ability, not only the use of the trigger finger
- ❑ Require thought and problem-solving skills
- ❑ Develop skills that will be carried into adult life and work
- ❑ Link the child to the culture of the real world
- ❑ Spur the child's curiosity and creativity

Six Family Activities for Dealing Effectively with Screen Violence

Activity 1: Counting and Discussing Violent Acts on the Screen
Introduction: This activity encourages children to consider the extreme violence encountered in many mainstream programs and films. Often children are simply not aware of the number of cruel acts they see on their favorite shows. By counting and discussing them, parents help their children become aware of screen violence and its glamorized portrayal.

Recommended age: Appropriate for any age

Instructions: Choose programs that your child enjoys watching. Instruct him that as he watches today, you would like him to count the number of acts that show physical harm to another person, an animal, or property. You may provide a list such as the following so that your child can put a check mark on the sheet whenever he sees such an act on the screen.

Type of Violence	Frequency
Hitting, punching	
Pushing, shoving	
Shooting, knifing	
Hurting an animal	
Destroying property	

After the program, tally up the number of violent acts and ask such questions as:

- Were you surprised with the number of violent acts? Why or why not?
- Did the show seem real to you? Why or why not?
- Would you like it if someone did these things to you?
- Which violent actions are used the most/least?
- What could the producer have done differently instead of using violent acts?
- Do the violent acts come at any particular times in the show, i.e., just before commercials?
- Who commits more violent acts? Men or women? Young or old? White or minority?
- Who is harmed by the violent acts? Men or women? Young or old? White or minority?

Continue discussing the program as long as your child shows an interest.

Activity 2: Rewriting Violent Scripts

Introduction: Too often the media send the message that violence is the best way to solve human problems. This activity will help teach children that there are a number of better ways to address problems.

Recommended age: Children of all ages can participate in this activity, though younger children will need help.

Instructions: As your child watches a program (cartoons are good for younger children), have him/her write down the basic problems the characters encounter and then write down the ways that the characters solve each problem.

After the program, have your child brainstorm ways in which people can address difficult situations without using violence. Discuss these ideas with the child. Then have your child act as a screenwriter or computer game program designer and use his own ideas to rewrite the plot. The goal is to eliminate the violence and come up with alternative solutions to the problems. Depending on the child's maturity and skills, this project can involve drawing pictures rather than writing. Or, the writing could consist of an outline. Have the child pay special attention to those elements that must be changed in order to eliminate the violence: Is it the people, the places, the time, the situation? Discuss your child's story with him and point out changes from the original.

Activity 3: Visualizing Different Heroes

Introduction: This activity exercises your child's creativity. It allows her to think about alternative images to the ones she sees daily on the screen. It also gives many children a sense of power and control.

Recommended age: Five to twelve

Instructions: Choose a TV program—one that your child is familiar with and enjoys watching—that contains violence. A cartoon works well for this activity. Tell your child that this time she will be doing a special activity as she watches.

Before the show begins, say something like: "When you watch this show, I want you to imagine another character being in the show—someone you make up from your own imagination. This person can be male or female, tall or short. The only thing you have to make sure of is that this person solves all his or her problems through talking, through negotiation, and through cooperation. *Never* through violence."

Once the character has been chosen, ask your child to describe the person and explain how s/he might act in a variety of situations. When the imagined character has been fleshed out, watch the show together and have your child imagine the character as part of the show. Ask questions like:

- ❑ What is your imagined character (IC) doing now?
- ❑ Does your IC like what is happening? Why or why not?
- ❑ What will your IC do next?

- ❑ Is the IC in the scene now? If not, where is he or she?
- ❑ Who does your IC like best? Least? Why?
- ❑ What makes him or her excited, bored, sad, happy?
- ❑ What does your IC want to tell you about the show?

During your discussion, you may have to remind your child that the imaginary character never acts violently.

Activity 4: Predicting Violent Content

Introduction: Predicting which television programs, movies, and video games will be violent is a good exercise in critical thinking. Ranking shows by the frequency of violent acts and intensity of violence is also valuable.

Recommended age: Eight to teens. With the help of a parent, this activity can also be adapted for younger children.

Instructions: Using any TV schedule, have your child predict which shows will have violence in them just by reading the titles. Go through a week's worth of programs and have him choose the five he thinks will be the most violent. Ask him to explain why he has selected these five particular shows. Depending on the programs, you and your child can plan to watch them together to assess his predictions.

For further comparison, look at a category of shows, such as movies, newscasts, docudramas, or sitcoms, and find out how many aired in a given week are very violent, somewhat violent, not very violent, or not at all violent. Collect this information in a table such as this one:

Program title	Much violence	Some violence	Little violence	No violence
Program one				
Program two				
Program three				

Activity 5: Comparing Media Violence Past and Present

Introduction: This activity gives older children and teens a historical perspective on media violence. It is an eye-opener even for adults. By understanding that media violence grows more and more intense in order to attract attention, your child will have one of the most sophisticated media literacy skills possible. We recommend that you do this activity several times with different types of television programs.

Recommended age: Eleven through teens

Instructions: Choose a TV program from the fifties or sixties and one from the nineties to compare. Some suggestions are *The Bugs Bunny Show* (this prime-time show ran on television from 1960 to 1962) with *Power Rangers* or *Star Trek* with *Deep Space Nine.* Have your child watch the two shows back-to-back if possible. As she watches, instruct her to make notes on a chart similar to this one:

	Older programs	Recent programs
Violence		
Number of violent acts		
Plot content		
Pace of action		
Music		
Special effects		

Your child will jot down words or phrases about each category as she watches the programs. Afterwards, discuss the responses on the chart, asking her what was most significant about the differences.

Activity 6: Understanding Meaningful Violence

Introduction: This activity may help children understand that not all violence is bad and that in many cases it serves to impart important messages. Distinguishing between glamorized violence and meaningful violence is a critical skill; it will help children recognize whether a producer is sensitively depicting the human condition or exploiting it.

Recommended age: Twelve through teens

Instructions: Select two different films or TV programs—one that uses violence sensitively and one that glamorizes it. One possibility would be the two films starring Denzel Washington, *Malcolm X* and *Ricochet.*

Explain to your child that this is an educational experience and that the purpose of watching the two movies is to analyze how the violence is portrayed in each. Watch both movies within two to four days if possible.

After you have watched both films together, ask your child to discuss the differences and similarities he has observed. The following questions may help draw out his ideas:

- How did you feel during the violent acts of each film? Any differences? Why or why not?
- Which film was cheaper to make? Can you tell? How?
- What emotions did the violence in each film evoke?
- Which film had the better acting? The better technical effects?
- Which film made you think more closely about the plot? Why?
- If you were to rewrite either or both of these films, what changes would you make?

Spend some time over several days talking about the two films or programs. The next time you watch a TV program or a movie with your child, ask what he thinks about the violence, if there is any. Can he tell the difference between a sensitive and a glamorized portrayal of violence?

4

The Coin of the Realm: Screen Advertising

The lights are low, the music a beguiling mix of hot rock and rap. Long-haired, sexy, young women eye the stupendously built, toweringly tall men as they strut their stuff—superhumans on a basketball court. For sixty seconds, the camera speeds between beautiful faces and athletic bodies, confounding the mind and arousing the emotions. The tempo builds, the spotlight narrows, the camera zooms, and there he stands—*Mr. Superstar.* As the camera moves from his face down to his feet, we get the message loud and clear: It's the shoes that put him in the spotlight! The shoes make him a superstar! Screen ads have taken boys' athletic footwear to a mystical level. What began as a lowly tennis shoe took on such grandiose importance for America's youth that by the early 1990s, a pair of sports shoes had become the motive for robbery, assault, and even murder.[1]

How Did Shoes Become So Important?

Psychology experts recognize the advertising industry as one of the most powerful socializing forces in our country. In fact, television programming exists solely because advertising revenue makes it so. Establishing sports heroes as product peddlers is one example of how the advertising industry influences young people's attitudes and behaviors. Whatever it takes to transform that star athlete into a hero will be done in order to sell more shoes. With this kind of promotional hype, is it any wonder that many American boys place such importance on certain brands of expensive athletic shoes?

Conscious Manipulation, Unconscious Decisions

Much of advertising's power lies in its ability to persuade on subliminal levels. Motivational research in the fifties found that most people were motivated from two basic needs—sex and security. So ads were designed to link products with the fulfillment of those needs. Insights from psychiatry and the social sciences were used to determine how best to attract a viewing audience. In 1969, the adman Herbert Krugman hooked his secretary up to a monitor only to discover that, while watching TV, the brain's cerebral cortex uses a different type of brain wave. Instead of being in the alert thinking state known as beta brain wave, the brain slips to the less active alpha state, in which it doesn't actively process information from the outside world.[2]

It wouldn't be an overstatement to say that for the past twenty-five years the advertising industry has known more about the workings of the brain than does the average American. The fast-paced, colorful images of commercials keep active thinking to a minimum. They hook the viewer by arousing strong emotions or fears. Commercials create quick impressions and influence us to link a product with a particular feeling or a particular perception about ourselves or our world. Children are particularly vulnerable to this conditioning.

Immunizing Children against Visual Sales Pitches

The average American child watches approximately 20,000 commercials each year.[3] Over time, an unrelenting barrage of screen advertising cumulatively affects children's development. Research supported by the National Science Foundation indicates that many children do not understand the selling intent of commercials, cannot distinguish them from the programs, and cannot explain their purpose.[4] However, with media literacy skills, children begin to question commercial messages and to critically examine what they view. As they become knowledgeable about advertising techniques, they come to understand the purpose of commercials. Consequently, they are less affected by them.

The Basic Screen Advertising Techniques

Below we examine six basic screen advertising techniques that you can identify for your children as you watch commercials with them. Following each technique is an activity that you may want to try out with your child.

A Fast Pace Grabs Our Attention and Hinders Our Ability to Evaluate Messages

A typical screen ad for a children's toy will have scene changes every two or three seconds. Fast-moving images hinder children's ability to reason yet keep them watching. Children equate "faster" with "more exciting," which is why commercials often seem more interesting to them than the programming.

Fast-paced activity: To help your child understand the style of fast-paced commercials, ask her to tap on the floor every time an image or a scene changes. Older children can count them or use a stopwatch to denote the time between changes.

Selling the Image, Not the Product

Advertisers promise beauty, popularity, sex appeal, love, eternal youth, superstar status, total fulfillment—if only we buy and use the miraculous product. Why else would an eight-year-old child insist on buying the exact, "right" brand of shoe? Image-making is ingrained in the American advertising industry.

Many people are surprised to learn that in Finland a court ordered McDonald's to take one of their commercials off the air. The ad showed a boy who was unhappy about moving to a new home. Suddenly he spied a McDonald's across the street and his mood changed to happy contentment. The Finnish court ruled that the commercial "falsely leads people to believe that a Big Mac can replace friends and ease loneliness."[5]

Marketing the image instead of the product is a form of institutionalized lying. Writing about TV advertising in our society, Charles Johnson and David Moore observe: "Advertising as conventionally practiced is a form of manipulation—put less kindly, lying. We all

Images and the Brain

With No Discussion

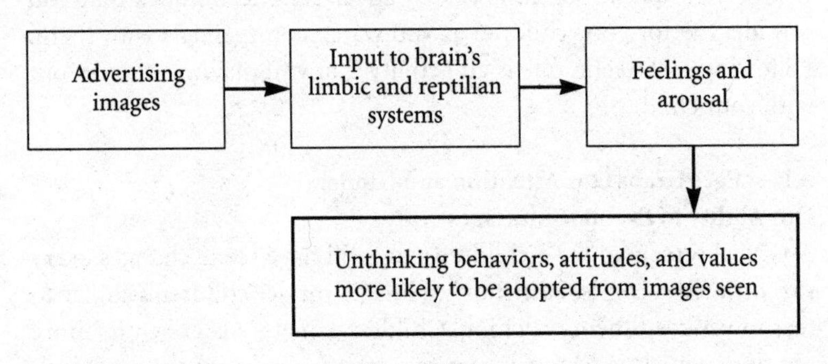

With Discussion

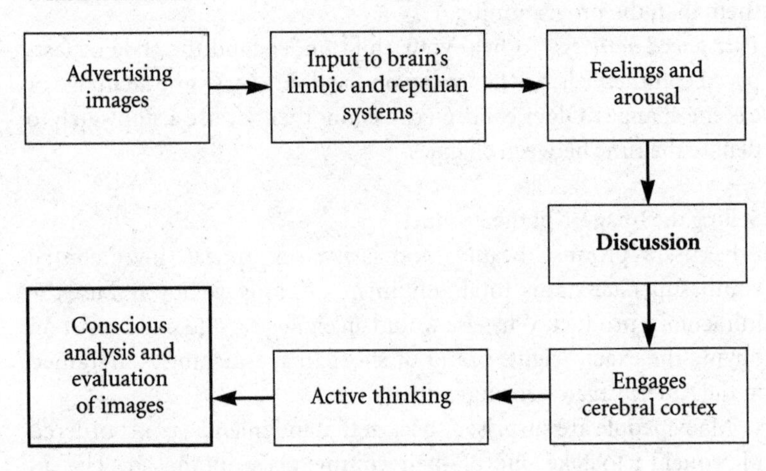

know we are being lied to, but interestingly this doesn't seem to diminish the effect. Advertising's power comes from the place it speaks to in our psyches. It uses the language of art and spirit—metaphor, image, movement, sound ... it plays off the subjective states of our deepest hopes and desires ... Rather than enabling the soul, its task is to deceive it."[6]

Discuss commercial images: After your child has watched a favorite commercial, ask questions: Do the people look like people you know?

Are the people doing things that ordinary people do? What are you learning about the product as you watch? How do the screen pictures make you feel? How do you think the writers of the commercial want you to feel?

Catchy Jingles Keep the Message Alive

Children are particularly good at remembering the catchy jingles, phrases, and tunes that go with TV commercials. Advertisers target this strength—they know that subject matter is more easily and more enjoyably learned through rhyme, rhythm, and music. It adds a distinct dimension to TV advertising, setting a mood that manipulates emotions.

Jingle activity: Have your child identify the repetitive words and phrases sung on a favorite commercial. Then ask your child why she thinks such a phrase or song is being repeated. What is actually being sold? Is it the product or is it a feeling? How does the jingle help a person remember the product? Ask your child if she knows any jingles from other commercials. If so, you may want to discuss those as well.

Popular People Make the Product Popular

A spokesman for Bausch and Lomb, the maker of Ray-Ban sunglasses, states, "When Andre Agassi became a teen idol ... we were swarmed by kids asking for the kind of Ray-Bans he wears."[7] Using celebrities to sell products is a popular advertising method because it has been proven successful. Endorsements by popular people encourage children to want the product more for its status appeal than for its utility.

Celebrity endorsement activity: Explain to your child what an endorsement commercial is. Then for the next week or so as you watch TV, identify these commercials for your child and pose questions: What are they selling? Is there any reason to think that the celebrities would know more than an average person about the product? Why or why not? How much do you think the celebrity is being paid to make this endorsement? How many times do you think the celebrity has used this product? Why do celebrity endorsement commercials work?

Camera Tricks Create Hype

The camera's eye is a marvel—it tells one version from one angle and another version from a different angle. For instance, in music videos, the camera usually surveys women from the bottom up, roaming slowly and languidly over female body parts. Men, on the other hand, are shown looking directly into the camera, eyeing it confidently. The camera less often landscapes a man's body, seldom objectifying him. Music videos have been studied and researched in order to prove that the differences in camera angles play a significant role in how men and women are perceived.[8]

Commercials, like music videos, consist of camera tricks that convey extremely important messages. For instance, in many commercials aimed at children, the camera angle is pitched looking up, mimicking a child's view of the world. Close-ups make products look bigger and more important. Strolling down an aisle in a toy store, we heard one child complain to his father, "But on TV it looked so big! Where's the big one?" The father patiently explained to his disappointed son that toy advertisers often make the toys look much bigger on television than they actually are.

How the camera relays commercial messages determines to a large degree what emotions and impressions are communicated. Although many adults ignore or mute commercials, children enjoy watching clever camera tricks. One woman related this incident:

> I was visiting my sister and her two-year-old child. We'd turned the TV on to catch the noon weather report. Jaime was playing with some blocks near the TV set and didn't pay much attention to the newscast itself. However, the second the commercials came on, Jaime's head would pop up and her eyes would fixate on the TV set. When the commercials were over, she'd return to her blocks. We watched it happen three or four times. It was amazing.

Camera-trick activity: Ask your child to mimic the role of the camera in a TV commercial. What, specifically, is revealed by the lens? What isn't being shown? Is the camera close to its subject? Is it far away? Does it move fast? Is it focused? Is it zooming? Discuss how the camera tricks contribute to the commercial's message and mood.

Special Props Make the Ideal Look Even Better

What we see on a commercial isn't always what's there. In cereal commercials, for instance, we think we see milk. But, in actuality, white glue is poured on the cereal because under bright lights milk gives off a bluish tint that doesn't look appetizing. A cup of cocoa looks steaming and delicious because detergent bubbles have been placed on the surface.[9] Producers of TV commercials use many false materials to make products look appealing on camera. Props are used to enhance an image, not to duplicate reality.

Props activity: Buy a product you know your child sees advertised on TV, such as a certain brand of cereal. With your child, examine the packaging and its contents. Does it look like it does on TV? What are the similarities and differences? Discuss the concept of enhancement with your child and why the product probably looks more appealing on TV. The next time you see the commercial for this product, point out any special props, such as the unblemished fruit accompanying the breakfast, that make the product look more attractive.

Screen Advertising Intentionally Targets Children

The four major networks—ABC, NBC, CBS, and Fox—spend more than $11 billion annually on advertising.[10] American children aged four to eighteen have a combined yearly allowance of $70 billion—about the same amount of money as Finland's gross domestic product.[11] Because of this spending power, American youths constitute a lucrative market. James McNeal, professor of marketing at Texas A&M University, points out that children are really three markets in one: "They are a current market . . . they are a future market . . . [and they] also constitute a market of influentials who cause many billions of dollars of purchases among their parents."[12]

Over the past decade, the advertising industry has in effect declared open season on children. Industry magazines such as *Advertising Age* and *Marketing Magazine* run regular features that detail strategies for selling to children's vulnerabilities. Articles such as "Easy Ways to Make Kids Notice the Message" and "Understanding the Child Consumer" instruct how best to reach the innocent mind.[13]

With research conclusions in hand, advertisers carefully design campaigns to sell to specific groups of children, segmenting the child market into smaller and smaller sections, such as preschoolers, children aged six to eight, children aged nine to eleven, preteens, teens. An example of this is the development of a new target group by the industry—the "tweens"—older children who are not yet adolescents. The larger number of audience groups that can be created, the more products can be sold. As soon as the five-year-old turns six, the beloved toy becomes obsolete in favor of a newer model, one targeted for his new peer group. Planned obsolescence intentionally keeps parents and children buying more and more products as the children grow.

Screen Advertising Creates Needs

As any parent knows, once a child wants something, s/he nags unmercifully for it. It's very difficult, especially when we're tired, to resist their whining. When children see toys advertised that are "in" with their peer group and start asking for them, we have our work cut out for us if we don't think the toy is appropriate and don't want to spend money on it. Even very young children can exert considerable pressure. A study conducted in a supermarket demonstrated that preschool children attempted to influence their mothers' purchases approximately once every two minutes, primarily for candy and sugared cereals. And not surprisingly, the children who watched more commercials made more requests for purchases.[14] Repetitive exposure to screen advertising can turn our children's wants into urgent *needs.*

The pressure that children put on their parents more often than not leads to parent-child struggles and energy-consuming squabbles. By craftily portraying products as necessary, advertisers lead children to think that it is the child's right to own the product. The child no longer merely *wants* something, the child *demands* something. The best and probably only lasting solution is to regularly explain to your child what the advertising industry's purpose is and what its motives are. Incidental questions as simple as the following can be effective: "That commercial certainly is trying hard to get people to buy the product. Does it make you want it?" "Boy, I think I'll buy those shoes and then I'll become a basketball star. What do you think?"

Children Are Apt to Believe Commercial Messages

Children have a difficult time believing that adults would deceive them. They take what is said at face value. Their naiveté is due to the fact that they lack adequate experience to make reasonable judgments. So when a favorite athlete or cartoon character says, "This will make you strong," it is too much to expect that a child will question the breakfast's nutritional value. Without adult guidance, the child is left believing that a partial truth is the whole truth.

Over the past decade, food commercials aimed at children have been extremely successful because they repeat similar, distorted messages about health and nutrition. A major study revealed that of 222 food commercials that were run on a Saturday morning, more than 90 percent promoted sugary cereals, candy bars, potato chips, and fast-food meals—a diet that is the opposite of what the Surgeon General recommends.[15] It is no coincidence that children's consumption of sugar and fat is increasing, as are health-related problems. Children's food ads are in reality *junk*-food ads.

Valid information about nutrition and how to understand it in relation to food products simply does not exist on commercial television. But rather than lament this fact, parents can use food ads as a way to steer the child in the direction of both media literacy and nutrition literacy. By comparing how a food item is advertised on television to its actual nutritional value, a child learns not only that the advertising industry is quite capable of exploiting its young audience, but also about the specific techniques that it uses to do so. Thrown into the bargain, the child learns about nutrition.

How Visual Messages Condition the Brain

Visual images travel directly into our thought processes. And once we have an image in our heads, it is very difficult to eradicate it. Advertisers view their "training" of children as their highest priority because once images are imbedded, they directly influence children's desires and behaviors for the rest of their lives. Images that children easily relate to are used extensively—for instance, animated characters are used in more than 40 percent of all commercials directed at young children.[16]

Although older children and young adolescents have the capabilities to better understand commercial messages, they are still affected in significant ways: Children aged nine to fourteen can develop loyalty to a product that lasts a lifetime. The advertising industry uses young teens' loyalty to condition their future buying behaviors. For instance, beer commercials use imagery designed to appeal specifically to eleven- to fourteen-year-old males. Research indicates that children who pay the most attention to beer commercials are the ones most likely to drink as adults.[17] In a California study on alcohol that concerned the opinions of fifth and sixth graders, it was found that the children who were more knowledgeable about beer ads also held more positive beliefs about drinking. A striking 88 percent of the children could identify Spuds MacKenzie and correctly link him with Bud Light.[18] Children who pay the most attention to commercials are the least likely to be skeptical about them.

Children Use Commercial Messages to Understand Their World
Continual visual sales pitches present a view of the world that advocates materialism as supremely important. Children learn to place inordinate value on material wealth at a time when they lack the mature thinking skills and worldly experience to combat these powerful messages. Commercials that appeal to youngsters' vulnerable emotional states significantly affect what they learn to value as they mature into adulthood.

Children and the Commercial Future

Screen advertising will only increase as technology advances. Thirty-minute infomercials, for instance, will become standard as the number of marketing channels increases. The sales pitch is not always immediately distinguishable from regular programming. Many adults admit to having been "suckered" into watching an infomercial for several minutes before they figured out it was a commercial. If adults have difficulty with this, imagine how confusing it must be for children.

The future also holds in store more "marketing programs" specifically designed to promote a product. For instance, "The Lion King: A Musical Journey," a television special, was broadcast a day after the movie *The Lion King* was released at the box office. The TV program was a behind-the-scenes look at the making of the music in the animated film and was produced in association with Disney television. Children tuning in to the program were going to be persuaded to see the movie, just in case they hadn't already decided they wanted to see it. Michael Jacobson, cofounder of the Center for the Study of Commercialism, said, "What these specials are is a subtle form of advertising. It's powerful because we're not told it's advertising. There's no pitchman, no ordering opportunities. But viewers should know that what they're watching is basically an infomercial . . ."[19]

We encourage parents to make it a habit to talk with children about screen advertising as much as they talk about other programming. Because parents cannot remake commercials that they feel aren't in the best interests of their children, their choices narrow to two when addressing the issue of screen advertising: 1) Monitor children's viewing and make sure they watch only what you want them to; 2) Teach children to understand the real messages that commercials are sending. That is what media literacy is all about.

Six Family Activities That Effectively Address Screen Advertising

Activity 1: Logging and Discussing Commercials

Introduction: This activity educates children about the world of television advertising. By keeping a chart and discussing it with parents, they learn how commercials are interwoven into the programming they watch; they learn to recognize products advertised; and they learn the ways in which commercials are designed to hook children's attention. By discussing their observations, children learn how advertising is meant to work.

Recommended age: Appropriate for any age. Younger children will need more assistance with the observation chart.

Instructions: Choose a program your child enjoys watching. Instruct her that as she watches today, she will fill in a chart similar to the one below about the commercials that she sees during the program. Explain to her that when a commercial comes on, she will write down the product being advertised in the "Product" column, and she will write a brief description of the commercial content under the column "What Happens." As children fill in the "What Happens" column, ask them to include a tally of the male/female characters, different ethnic and racial characters, and ages. Afterwards they can discuss their reactions to the information they've gathered.

You may have to cue the child as to when the commercials begin. At the end of the program, turn off the television. Use the questions below as general guidelines in your discussion:

- How did the commercial make you feel?
- What caught your interest in this commercial?
- Could what happened on the commercial happen in real life? Why or why not?
- What did you learn about the product advertised? Would you need more information about the product in order to buy it?
- Were the commercials louder and/or faster than the program? If so, why do you think they made it that way?
- Did you have to pay a lot of attention to understand what was happening? Or was it easy to pay attention to the commercial?
- Was it easier to watch the commercial than it was to watch the program? Why or why not?
- Who is the commercial made for? Would this commercial sell the product to a child? To a teen? To an adult? What would you do to change the commercial to sell the product to someone else?
- If you were making this commercial, would you change anything about it? What? Why?

Activity 2: Imaginative Advertising

Introduction: In this activity, young children learn to spot identifiable characters to better understand how celebrity endorsement works. Learning this in early childhood can help children be alert to advertising manipulation later on. Working with cartoons and fairy tale characters is a fun and nonthreatening way for them to learn this lesson.

Recommended age: Four to seven

Instructions: First, brainstorm with your child various cartoon and fairy tale characters. Pick her favorite, and then talk with her about the personality, activities, and unique traits of the character. Using this information, together pick an item or product that would be reasonable for the character to advertise, such as Mickey Mouse and cheese; Cinderella and shoes; Jack and bean seeds; Humpty Dumpty and eggs.

After the item is chosen, discuss the following questions:

- What will the character say about his or her product?
- How does the character look?
- Would you buy the product from this character? Do you think other people would? Why or why not?

After this discussion, have the child draw a picture of the character selling his or her product.

Activity 3: Distinguishing Fantasy from Real Life

Introduction: This activity helps children distinguish the fantasy elements of commercials and the true qualities of actual products. By comparing what they see on the screen to real consumer items, they begin to differentiate advertising gimmicks from true facts. There are several steps to this activity, and we encourage you to follow them in order for best results.

Recommended age: Five and older

Instructions:

Step 1: Watch a commercial with your child about a product he is interested in. If possible, tape the commercial for future use. Discuss the commercial with him, using similar questions to those in Activity 1.

Step 2: Discuss with your child his expectations about this product. Some questions you may want to ask are:

- What do you think the product will look like?
- How do you think the product will perform?
- Will the product look different when you see it in the store? Why or why not?
- How much will the product cost?
- Did the commercial make you want to buy the product? Why or why not?

Step 3: Buy the product with your child and try it out with him: If it's food, eat it; if it's a toy, play with it; and so on. After you've done this, play the taped version of the commercial to remind your child how the product looked on the screen. Then discuss the following questions with him:

- ❑ Does the product look the same in real life?
- ❑ What are the major differences?
- ❑ Does the product act in the same way as it did on TV? What did you notice on TV that did not happen when you tried the product?
- ❑ What information was left out of the commercial that you think is important?
- ❑ Do you think the commercial gave you adequate information about the product? Why or why not?
- ❑ If you were creating this commercial, how would you change it so people would get better information about the product?

Step 4: Decide with your child if this product is of enough value to keep. If not, would he return it and get his money back? Why or why not?

Activity 4: Observing Body Language in Commercials
Introduction: This activity helps children learn how to interpret subtle and hidden messages in commercials. Children will need to observe carefully as the actors convey messages through body language —eye contact, sexualized movements, facial expressions, postures, gestures, head positions. They then will practice their reasoning skills to link the observed body language with the more subtle commercial message.

Recommended age: Seven and older

Instructions: Have your child watch several commercials that show people involved in various activities. Have them point out the different ways the actors use their bodies. You probably will have to draw out specific information from the child. For instance, if she tells you that she saw somebody running, ask how they were running—quickly, slowly, hesitantly—and how they looked while they were running—happy, afraid, eager, tired. The more specific the information, the easier it will be for the child to make a link between the body language and the commercial message.

After you've identified several different movements of the actors, discuss with your child some of the following questions:

- What story is being told by the body movement? What does the body movement tell you the product will do for you?
- How do the actors' body movements and positions affect how you feel about the product?
- For each body movement that your child has observed, ask how the commercial might differ if that body movement were taken out. Would the message be the same? Why or why not?

Activity 5: Understanding Audience Appeal

Introduction: With this activity, children learn that advertisers use a number of stock appeals to influence their audience. By identifying the appeals and then discussing and comparing them, the child begins to acquire a sophisticated response to advertising techniques.

Recommended age: Nine and older

Instructions: The following list illustrates the main types of audience appeal. Have your child watch commercials until he has collected appeals in each category.

Types of Audience Appeal

- Factual appearance: A businesslike appeal; numbers are questionable
- Comparison: The product is the best compared to others
- Testimonial: Trustworthy people swear by the product
- Clever production: Dazzles the audience with fanfare, dramatics, or exaggerations
- Bargains: Who can turn down a bargain?
- Integrity: Links honesty and strength of character with the product
- Soft sell: Charms the viewers or persuades through understatement
- Popularity: Appeals to our desire to belong to a group

- Bandwagon: Everybody is using it
- Glittery generalities: Talks a lot without saying anything
- Transfer: X buys it, and I'll be more like X if I buy it
- Putdown: Denigrates another product, usually unnamed

After the child has identified most of these appeals, discuss how they work to persuade people to buy products. Which one does your child think works best on her? Why? Are there any that she thinks wouldn't work at all? Why not?

Ask the child to consider which audiences would be susceptible to the different types of appeal. For instance, would teens be more easily persuaded by an appeal to popularity? Would a very young child be impressed with a popular basketball player selling shoes?

Ask older children what they think about these manipulations. Is manipulation fair? Is it necessary? Why does it seem to work? Ask the question: Do you think that most of the people being appealed to in these specific ways are conscious of it? Why or why not?

Activity 6: Studying Advertising Patterns

Introduction: In this activity, children have the opportunity to create their own commercials as they learn about different audience appeals and specific advertising patterns. The child should be encouraged to come up with original ideas; there are no right or wrong answers in this activity.

Recommended age: Nine and older

Instructions: Have the child think of two products, real or imaginary, that could be advertised during each of the following programs:

- basketball game
- daytime soap opera
- evening news
- cartoon show
- golf tournament
- cop show
- game show
- family comedy

After your child has selected her products, she then designs a commercial for one of them. Tell her to keep in mind which audience she is trying to reach with this commercial. She may write a script, draw pictures, or role-play the commercial for you. Follow her presentation with a discussion about her reasons for designing the commercial the way she did: Why does she think it will reach her audience? Is there anything special she did to make sure it would?

5

The Show's the Thing! News and Talk Shows

We've never found a clearer explanation of what is needed for children regarding TV news and talk shows than these wise words from a pioneer of television news, Walter Cronkite: "I have advocated for thirty years that, in order to preserve our democracy and protect ourselves against demagogues, we should have courses in schools on how to watch TV, how to read newspapers, how to analyze a speech, how to understand the limitations of each medium and make a judgment as to the accuracy or the motives involved. We should be curious enough to seek further information, to know that there are gaps in the information being presented. What is really required, I think, is *multi*media education."[1]

Acquiring accurate information on what is happening in our communities, our country, and the world has become increasingly difficult in this age of screens. For, despite the many hours of news programming available to us, the definition of "important information" has changed. Sifting through what *poses* as newsworthy to find what *is* newsworthy becomes more and more necessary. Separating fact from opinion and media hype from actual news is a crucial media literacy skill for children and adults alike.

The fact that we receive more information doesn't always mean that we are better informed. Telephone books and computer databases give us a tremendous amount of information, but the information must be used correctly, with a specific purpose in mind. Seldom does a person spend an hour randomly flipping through a phone book. Yet television news and talk shows are often turned on automatically, out of habit.

Today it is more important than ever to watch news *intentionally*, because too often there is missing or misconstrued information. In a recent poll of eight nations, it was found that Americans knew less about current events than did the citizens of the other seven nations. In a series of five questions, 37 percent of Americans answered all of the questions incorrectly, while only 3 percent of the Germans missed all the questions.[2] In fact, studies reveal that American children who watch a good deal of television are *less* informed about the world than their counterparts who watch little or none.[3] In *How to Watch TV News*, Neil Postman and Steve Powers observe: "Americans have rapidly become the least knowledgeable people in the industrialized world. We know *of* many things (everything is revealed) but *about* very little (nothing is known)."[4]

TV News Today

Television is run by corporations with the single pursuit of making as much money as possible. Today the costs of television programming are skyrocketing and there is strong, new competition from cable, video, and other popular forms of entertainment. The result? Reduced industry profits. Yet driven to maintain profit margins, corporations have discovered that TV news programs are moneymakers: Every night, more than *40 million* adults watch television news programs. Being "informed" has become a favorite obsession, and more than 60 percent of the American public relies on TV news as their *sole* source of information about the world.[5]

News programs are much less expensive to produce than entertainment programs. And while large profits make the broadcast corporations and the advertisers happy, what about the viewers who want solid news coverage?

Even insiders understand the problem. Reuven Frank, former president of NBC News, says, "The news business is no longer the news business. Now it's just a business like any other."[6] It's not accidental that television news has come to be called TV news *shows*.

Television news now relies heavily on glitz and superficialities. More money than ever is being spent on wardrobe, makeup, and sets. Increasingly, image is more important than substance. CBS Evening News uses video cameras equipped with the latest "skin contour" technology, providing on-air face lifts that give the news anchors and guests wrinkle- and blemish-free appearances.

Packaging the news like entertainment—quick, trivial, and sensational—captures the attention of the largest number of people. However, viewers aren't receiving thorough coverage, since most news stories last only forty-five to ninety seconds.[7] Yet most Americans watch every night in order to stay informed. In his now classic book, *Amusing Ourselves to Death,* Neil Postman writes: "No matter what is depicted [on TV] . . . the overarching presumption is that it is there for our amusement and pleasure. That is why even on news shows, which provide us daily with fragments of tragedy and barbarism, we are urged by the newscasters to 'join them tomorrow.' What for? One would think that several minutes of murder and mayhem would suffice as material for a month of sleepless nights."[8] When the real issues are disguised as mindless entertainment, they become lost.

Television news is good at creating the need for more news. For example, during the Gulf War, the twenty-four-hour coverage brought to our living rooms a constant stream of the most mundane details and trivial matters. But did all those hours of news contribute to our understanding of the issues? Did they actually deliver news or did they simply fill our time and zap our energy? Were the viewers who watched around the clock better informed than those who watched thirty minutes or less a night and read newspapers and magazines during the course of events? By creating a deluge of information packaged for easy digestion, the television industry has created the dangerous illusion that the more time we spend watching hyped, sensational images delivered in information sound bites, the better informed we are.

Screen Information and Children and Adolescents

Millions of today's children and teens turn on the television when they wake up in the morning, as soon as they get home from school in the afternoon, when they eat their dinner, and finally, in the evening, while they (try to) do their homework. They will find themselves unintentionally watching a great amount of television news and talk shows—programming that by its very nature is often not suitable for them.

If you want to know how TV news and/or talk shows might affect your children, try to watch a full newscast or a talk show, uninterrupted by anyone or anything, pretending that you're the same age as your child. Imagine that you don't know much about history, so you aren't able to put the events you're seeing into a larger context or view them from another perspective. Remember, too, that you don't have the verbal sophistication to understand all of the ideas presented. Remind yourself often that your child might respond to visual images as if they were real. And remember that everything—*everything*—you see and hear, you believe is the *whole* truth.

What was the outcome? If you're like most parents, you are surprised to learn how different this viewing experience is from what your own would have been. What are your thoughts on the amount of violence, disaster, and generally negative coverage? Do you feel somewhat confused, disoriented, and helpless? Use these insights to help your child make sense of the information that's presented on the screen. The content that most needs to be interpreted for young people is that found in news programs and talk shows: These programs call for extreme parental vigilance and monitoring. The younger the child, the more regulation needed.

The following five reasons might encourage you to set limits on news and talk shows:

Much of what is covered on television news involves the most negative aspects of human behavior. Children don't understand that news programs offer a very narrow view of what is actually happening in the world. How often have you heard an adult complain that TV news focuses on negative events and tragedy? Adults base their complaints on a knowledge of a wide variety of human behavior and accumulated experiences. Adults understand that talk shows don't present a balanced view of real life. But children are less able to see this. Without the benefit of years of learning and experiences, they are much more likely to misinterpret information.

Distinguishing screen fact from opinion can be difficult for children and teens. Children usually have difficulty determining that a story may be reported in a slanted way, or that a news anchor, by a deliberate inflection of voice or facial expression, can bias what should be an unbiased report. Even when such subtleties are pointed out to them, they often cannot grasp the difference between straight news reporting and editorializing. Entirely erroneous information and people's opinions may seem like fact to them.

Messages and stories absorbed at an early age are the most impactful to children. If violent, bizarre stories are framing children's perceptions of life, they are more likely to grow up with distorted images of reality. For instance, multiple stories about youth gangs might cause children to believe that most youth of a certain age or race are involved in gangs. Sensational talk shows send skewed and harmful messages about how people are supposed to behave. If these types of programs convey the first cultural messages, children are likely to compare all future accounts, no matter how realistic, to these inaccurate ones.

Children and teens are attracted to glitz and the sensational. Kids are attracted to hyped stimuli, and if they are exposed to too much of it, they may come to believe that hype *must* be present for information to be worthwhile and interesting. Impressionable young minds cannot determine what is and what isn't newsworthy amid all the packaging. For instance, one significant way the broadcasting industry tries to persuade us to watch news programs is by running ten-second blurbs—commercials for TV news and news magazines. Known as "teases," these promos often appear during family prime-time viewing, inviting us, as appealingly as possible, to "join them" for their broadcast. Short clips featuring the most sensational story of the day or week are meant to entice viewers, and they frequently depend on violence and sex to get viewers' attention. A friend tells us of an experience that drove her to write a scathing letter to the local station:

> The exquisite movie *Dances with Wolves* had just ended. My children were feeling the pain, the hardship of those last moving scenes. The names of the cast started up on the TV set. In no more than three sec-

onds, the insistent voice of the local female anchor blared out: "A woman mutilates her husband by cutting off his penis. Will justice be delivered? Join us at eleven to find out." I was livid, my kids looked embarrassed, and the beauty of the movie's ending was lost for us.

Kids become fearful when information is presented out of context. Many young children don't yet understand the concept of large numbers, long distances, time, or cause and effect. This puts them at a real disadvantage, particularly when they try to put the frightening stories they see on TV in perspective.

The 1993 earthquake in Los Angeles provided child experts a chance to see what effect the vivid screen coverage of the earthquake's devastation had on children. Dr. Robert B. Brooks, a child psychologist who teaches at Harvard University, said, "They're worried about what could happen to their house, even if they live thousands of miles away. After the television coverage of the bombing of Baghdad a few years ago, children in this country worried that their homes would be bombed in retaliation."[9] Other studies have found that after watching traumatizing news accounts, children continue to think about them and dream about them months later.

Older children and teens are equally affected by frightening news. For instance, if most of the stories about schools they see on television have to do with violence, it is only natural that they might begin to think that all schools are violent. They may even begin to fear going to school themselves.

Screen Information Readiness

When is a child ready to watch TV news and talk shows and evaluate them logically?

Ages Three through Five

Preschoolers definitely are *not* ready to watch TV news or talk shows. At this writing, there is no news program written for the three- to five-year-old set. And there shouldn't be. It is normal for children at this stage of development to be involved in their own environments.

It is a mistake to even have the evening news or a talk show on in a

Suggestions for Parents of Preschoolers

- Watch a later TV news program, when your child is asleep.
- If you want to watch the news or a talk show but your preschooler is playing nearby, cover the TV screen and simply listen to the broadcast. Your child will be much less attracted to only the sound. Or listen to radio news and tape the talk show for viewing when your child is asleep.
- Take turns—one night Mom watches and Dad spends time with the children—the next night you switch.
- Use newspapers and magazines as your primary source of information.

preschoolers' range of vision. For the young child, images are alive—they have power. Psychologists often use screen images to change toddlers' behavior, such as curing a fear of dogs by showing them films of a child playing happily with a dog. An interesting example illustrates the point: Psychologist Robert O'Connor selected the most severely socially withdrawn children from four preschools and showed them a film depicting a solitary child observing other children playing and then happily joining them. His findings are reported by Arthur Deikman in his book *The Wrong Way Home:* "After watching the film, the children immediately began to interact with their peers.... After six weeks ... they were leading their schools in amount of social activity. It seems that a 23-minute movie, viewed just once, was enough to reverse a potential pattern of lifelong maladaptive behavior."[10] If watching only twenty-three minutes can make this kind of an impact, imagine the effects on the preschooler of repeated exposure to violent news and the negative images which are so often found on talk shows.

Ages Six through Ten

Children in this age group may benefit from viewing carefully selected news programs that are designed especially for children their age—ones without violent images, if you can find them. They may encourage kids to begin thinking about the role of current events in their lives. But, as with preschoolers, there is no overwhelming reason they should regularly be watching TV news and talk shows produced for adults. One mother, an elementary school teacher, was surprised to learn that her nine-year-old son thought the John Bobbitt case was actually ten different cases around the country. He had heard about it so often on the evening news that he didn't understand that it was one isolated case receiving more than its share of notoriety. She was taken aback that even at the age of nine, her child could have such a misconception.

The world of adult TV news programs is too unknown and frightening a place for elementary school children. However, there are news shows designed specifically for children of this age. Linda Ellerbee's *Nick News* presents news to children in an appropriate and enticing way. Parents can watch along with their children, discussing important points. One parent, Inga, tells of watching *Nick News* with her daughter:

> I was curious to see what kind of news the industry thought would attract kids, so I took time that Sunday evening to sit with Laura and watch the show. To my surprise, I found myself really interested in the subjects they were covering and in the professional manner in which the kids were performing. The pacing seemed about right. Laura was pleased that I liked the same program she did; we had a good (and lengthy, for us) discussion about one of the stories we had watched together.

Taking the time to find these shows and making them part of your child's regular viewing are well worth the effort.

Ages Eleven through Fourteen

By age eleven or twelve, most kids will have developed the necessary language and thinking skills to make a pertinent analysis of news programs designed for their age group. Many teachers have found Channel One beneficial for engaging middle-school students in thoughtful discussions about the news. At home, kids can benefit by watching children's news programs designed specifically for them.

Much of the content of talk shows appeals to the early adolescent. While we don't advocate that children in this age group watch a lot of talk shows, or even news programs, we know that realistically they will probably see some of these programs. As parents, we can steer young teens away from the polarized treatment of sensational topics to more in-depth thought and analysis. If they feel they are old enough to watch these types of shows, then they are old enough to critique them and talk about them, too. There are ways to encourage junior high kids to think more critically about talk shows and news programs:

Provide an alternative fact-finding mission. If your young teen has watched a news or talk show about teen pregnancy, for example, have him or her research the facts given on the show. Were they correct? What information was missing? Your child may discover that a lot of important information is left out of the television coverage.

Conduct local interviews. Have your children find out what other adults think of a topic presented on a talk show by conducting interviews of adult family members, relatives, or neighbors. Point out to your child that when a person has gained some life experience, they tend to hold up information gained from a talk show in light of information learned firsthand. Usually a rich background of personal experiences puts the sensationalistic talk-show spin in its place. Through talking with a variety of adults, your child will become privy to new perspectives.

Write reactions and what was learned after watching. After viewing a talk show, have your child write down her feelings and two or three sentences summarizing what was learned. This allows you to monitor any distortions your child may have picked up while viewing and also provides a springboard for further conversation. In a discussion, point out media hype and review and respond to any antisocial behaviors your child may have seen. Set the story straight.

High school kids should be watching, talking, and thinking about selected news programs and news magazines. Much of their content can be a great starting point for discussing sensitive topics with your teen, providing a unique opportunity to expose teens to a broader view. For instance, if they're watching, thinking, and talking about starvation in Africa, their desire to wear the latest fashions might not seem so vitally important by comparison. More advanced, intelligent questioning of the screen information is essential for this age group. Here are examples of questions you can ask:

- Is this news story important enough to take up two minutes of 40 million people's time? Why or why not?
- Will watching the weird behavior on a talk show make other people want to behave in the same way? Why or why not? (Discuss copycat behavior and how it comes about.)
- How do you tell screen facts from screen opinions?
- If you were the talk show or news magazine host, how would you handle this guest?

Did you learn everything you needed to know about the subject from this show or story? What was missing? What could have been cut?

Six Family Activities for Dealing Effectively with News and Talk Shows

Activity 1: Keeping and Discussing a News Log

Introduction: With this activity your child will begin to see not only what's reported on TV news, but the many diverse elements that are brought together to produce a news broadcast.

Recommended age: Eight and older

Instructions: Choose a news program that is broadcast at a time convenient for you to view it for five days to a week. Explain to your child that as he watches the news he will record what he sees and learns on a chart like the one below:

	Subject	Violent	Peaceful	Positive	Negative	Neutral
Story 1						
Story 2						
Story 3						
Story 4						

The Problems with TV Talk Shows

- TV talk shows present an unbalanced view of life. They attract their audiences by using subject matter that is unfailingly sensational, more marginal, more negative, and more headline-grabbing than the issues that face most of us daily. These programs present a carnival world of weirdness and fringes.
- When we watch a TV talk show, we watch other people talking. We are not talking ourselves. We are not with the people closest to us—people in our families and our communities. We are isolating ourselves from the real world, letting talk shows fill our lives with their chatter.
- Talk shows are planned conflict. Though the hosts often claim that they serve the purpose of educating the public, too often they seem like Roman senators, pitting the lions against the slaves. They encourage verbal combativeness—it's exciting, and that makes for a "better" show. These hosts are more than willing to sacrifice rational discussion for hype. Rather than listening to intelligent exchanges about serious issues, we're left simply shaking our heads in helpless amazement.
- TV talk shows are memorable. Research indicates that emotional states affect how much information the mind retains. The more highly aroused or excited a person feels as they watch visual images, the better they will remember those images. Children respond especially well to the talk-show hype, remembering subjects they would have been better off forgetting.

To begin, he will write down every story covered by the news in the order they appear, starting with the first one. Examples would be "house fire," "store robbery," or "South American earthquake." After noting the story topic, he should think about the story, decide whether it is a violent or nonviolent subject, and record his decision.

Then he decides how he would categorize the story: positive, negative, or neutral. If he needs help understanding what category a story should fall into, demonstrate for him how you would label particular stories.

When your child has finished compiling his news log, you can use these questions to help him learn some important facts about TV news:

- What type of stories start off the show? Is there any pattern? If so, why?
- Many people think there is too much emphasis on violence in the TV news. Based on the information you've collected, do you think so? Why or why not?
- Are there as many positive stories on TV news as negative stories? Or are the majority of the stories neutral?
- If you were a news director, what story would you begin with? Why?
- If you were a news director, where would you put sports news: in the first half of the program, in the middle, or at the end? Why?
- What types of stories attract an audience for the news? Why do you think this is so?

Activity 2: What Do We Learn from the News?

Introduction: Why do we watch the news? Is it something that we really need, that we can really use, that will really help us? Children will begin to think about these issues as they do this activity.

Recommended age: Eight and older

Instructions: With your child, watch a news broadcast. After each story is aired, you and your child will individually record what you learned from the story. If you didn't learn anything, write that down.

When the newscast is concluded, share what you both recorded for each story. Point out the differences; highlight the similarities. Discuss how adults and children sometimes form different impressions of and learn different things from the stories they see on the TV news.

Next, discuss whether the information you both learned is important. Is there value in knowing that a schoolbus ran off the road in a distant state? How important is it to know that property taxes are increasing? Why?

Lastly, address the topic of whether the new information that you learned from this TV newscast will be information you remember. Ask your child if he would be more likely to remember something that he thought was important or unimportant. For how long will he remember? A day, a week, a month, a year? More? Why?

Have your child decide which of the stories contained information that could be important to remember. How could this information help? How could it be used? Would anything happen if this information was forgotten?

Activity 3: Comparing TV News Programs

Introduction: Children will learn that the news is presented in a number of different ways, and that what viewers learn varies depending on the way the news is presented. By comparing two different newscasts, both young and older children can learn a great deal.

Recommended age: Eight and older

Instructions: Instruct children to tape and watch two news programs aired on the same day at roughly the same time. You may have to enlist the help of a neighbor or friend to tape one of the programs. Then have the child compare the two newscasts: What are the similarities, the differences? Are the stories arranged differently? Is more or less time devoted to the same stories reported on the two stations? Compare the anchors, the reporters, the sets, the graphics, the chitchat, the number of special reports, and the commentaries. Older children can note the similarities and differences on paper; younger children can verbally report their observations or even draw pictures (of the two different sets, for example).

Activity 4: Rating the Effectiveness of News Presentation

Introduction: The ability to recognize and judge what elements make for a better news broadcast is an important skill for children to learn. This activity will help them mature from passive viewers into better judges of whether the information the television industry presents is newsworthy.

Recommended age: Eight and older

Instructions: Have your child watch several news programs and then fill out the chart below for each. Compare the final scores and ask him to explain why he thinks there were differences.

Poor	Fair	Average	Good	Very Good	Excellent
1	2	3	4	5	6

Assign a number to each element of the news program that you watched.

1. Variety of stories ___
2. Audience appeal ___
3. Appeal of the anchors ___
4. Appeal of the reporters ___
5. Knowledge of anchors ___
6. Knowledge of reporters ___
7. Fairness and lack of bias ___
8. Use of pictures ___
9. Use of background information ___
10. Total effectiveness (add all numbers together) ___

After your child has finished, talk with him about how he ranked the individual elements. Did the total effectiveness score reflect the overall quality of the news program?

Focus on those news programs to which he gave the lowest ratings. What changes would he make to improve those newscasts? Would the changes cost a lot of money? Could they be made fairly easily? Have him send his suggestions to the stations that broadcast the programs. The letter should be upbeat and thoughtful. (Address it to the News Director.) Your child can almost count on a personal response.

Activity 5: Putting on a Newscast

Introduction: There's nothing like being privy to knowledge that normally only an "insider" would have. Add to that the fact that television and acting are natural magnets for children, and you have a sure-fire hit: a kid-made news program. This is a good long-range activity; allow up to a week or two for the best results.

Recommended age: Eight and older. Older children can put together a complete news program, while younger children can report on just one or a few stories. This is a wonderful activity for a group of children, either siblings or friends.

Instructions: Your child, along with perhaps several other children, will be putting on a newscast. They can decide the content of the newscast in several ways: newspaper stories; neighborhood events; school activities and events. A major element of interest is added if they use a video camera and actually tape the newscast. It can be shown to family, relatives, friends, and school classes.

Parents should assign roles: director, producer, writers, anchors, weather reporter, sportscaster, camera people, sound director, art director, stage director, and so on. Decide which stories you will be covering in a meeting of all the "news staff."

These are some of the tasks that must be addressed:

- The director will assign all jobs — reporting, set design, wardrobe for anchors, artwork, on-location news gathering and filming.
- The producer will arrange the finished stories in order. The producer is also responsible for making up commercials that might run during the newscast. He can assign the making of the commercials to another staff person.
- The news director and the producer will work with the reporters and the camera person to edit the written and taped stories.

Rehearsal: The set director supervises a run-through of the show. This is a chance for the participants to get comfortable with being on camera, to check that the light is right, and to make sure that the stories read well. Make any changes necessary.

Taping: The camera person tapes the show. If video recording equipment isn't available, the children can perform their newscast in front of an audience, or record it on cassette.

Activity 6: What's Important to Know

Introduction: In this activity, children learn to distinguish differences among news stories covered at the local, national, and international levels. They are also learning to think creatively about the function of television news itself. Through watching and becoming aware of topics covered on TV news and by making up their own news topics, children begin to understand that being media literate involves deciding what is newsworthy and what isn't.

Recommended age: Ten and older

Instructions: Have your child watch several television news broadcasts within the course of a week. As she watches, ask her to keep track of the major topics covered pertaining to local, national, and international stories. After each program, with your help, she can fill out a chart similar to the one below:

Types of news	News show #1	News show #2	News show #3
Local news			
National news			
International news			

At the end of the week, ask her questions to help her reflect on the news topics she recorded:

- What are the topics for local, national, and international news? How are they similar? How are they different?
- Do you think the topics are important ones? Why or why not?
- What are the main topics covered? Are they given more coverage than you think appropriate? Why or why not?
- Which news program/s do you think gave the best coverage? Why?
- What important topics are missing from the news reports you watched? Why do you think this is so?

After your discussion, ask your child to make a list of the topics she thinks should be addressed on news programs due to their significance. Her list may or may not include topics consistently covered. Then have her write down five to ten topics and discuss with her the pros and cons of airing them on the news. Would her topics attract a viewing audience? Why or why not? Who would benefit from watching? How would she change a news program to make sure some of her topics were covered? How would she sell her creative ideas to the advertisers who sponsor the programs?

6

Typecast: Screen Stereotypes

An alien, stepping off her spaceship onto the strange planet earth and seeing TV for the first time, is going to draw some mistaken notions about life as we know it in America. What first confuses the alien is that few earthlings on television appear to be over the age of forty. She also sees that on TV there are few women as major characters: Men are the leaders. Puzzled, the alien looks for clues as to what humans do to make a living, and then draws the conclusion that most humans don't work. The observation that few characters on TV are gainfully employed leads the alien to further puzzlement: Why, then, are the vast majority of people portrayed on TV so well-off? Where do they get their money?

Since children take what they see at face value, their view of TV is very much like the alien's. They see what's on the screen and naturally interpret it as the way things are or are supposed to be. A study of children's television conducted by Dr. Katharine Heintz-Knowles at the University of Washington revealed that many children portrayed on commercial broadcast television and basic cable channels were living a life without parental or family ties—a life free of responsibilities, such as household chores and homework. The majority of TV children are white, and more than 40 percent of them are aged fourteen to eighteen.[1] Such stereotypes create serious problems for young viewers. In this chapter we examine the different types of media stereotyping, discuss how children are affected by them, and provide practical ways to educate children about them.

Screen Images of How We Live

Work

On television, most work is done by cops, lawyers, and medical personnel. Where are the office workers, the sales clerks, the computer programmers, the bus drivers? By seldom paying attention to these and the thousands of other real and necessary occupations, screens give a slanted view of the working world. Jobs shown on television usually carry a large paycheck and are typically carried out in dramatic settings: courtrooms, hospital emergency rooms, police departments. Research has shown that in the world of TV, professions such as doctor, lawyer, and law enforcer "far outnumber all other working people put together."[2]

Women characters who are employed usually work in traditionally female occupations—nursing, secretarial jobs, waitressing. Males outnumber females in all professional occupations, including real-life female-oriented careers, such as teaching. "In addition, married women [on the screen] are far less likely than married men to successfully mix marriage and child-rearing with careers. While nearly 60 percent of real married women also are employed outside their homes, only 26 percent of the employed women on television are or have been married."[3]

When a television character is shown "working," the viewer isn't shown what the work actually is. A real-life police officer relates the difference between police work on television and the work that policemen and women do in reality: "They never show TV cops filling out the mountains of paperwork that I have to do every day before I get my paycheck. Watching these cop shows can make a person, especially children, think that all we do is arrest drug addicts and chase murderers at a hundred miles an hour." In the same vein, nurses and doctors on television are never shown reading and conducting research, as they do in real life to keep their medical skills honed. Obviously these functions would not make for a dramatic script, but it's important for children to understand that these choices have been made.

Leisure

Though we don't see people working on television, we certainly see them playing. Wouldn't we all love having the seemingly unending supply of leisure time that most TV characters have? What's so often lacking is a sense of balance between work and play, community and family obligations—the real life of most Americans. And the recreational activities of screen characters at times reflect questionable behavior: smoking, alcohol, and drug use. Scenes showing these activities are interwoven into plots and character development.

A study by Stanton Glantz of the University of California in San Francisco analyzed 158 television comedies and dramas and concluded that 24 percent of the programs contained at least one shot of smoking, tobacco billboards, ashtrays, or smoke-filled rooms. Glantz's colleague, Anna Hazan, of the university's Institute for Health Policy Studies, raised the concern that the smoking by admired characters is sending the wrong message to impressionable youngsters. "By and large, smoking is presented as positive. . . . It may contribute . . . to the attitude that smoking is a socially desirable behavior."[4]

Like smoking, alcohol and drug consumption are also seen on television, but there the portrayal is beginning to change. Yes, there are still plenty of stereotypical images, especially in beer commercials, but there has been a concerted effort by the television industry to stop glamorizing alcohol and drug abuse. In 1986 the Academy of Television Arts and Sciences launched its campaign against substance abuse by setting up guidelines for television portrayal of drug and alcohol abuse.[5] However, adherence to the guidelines is voluntary. Therefore, the fun aspects of drugs or alcohol are still larger than life, while the hangovers, the pain of addiction, the drunk driving arrests, the violence and abuse, and the health problems are less evident. Television specials that set the story straight about drug and alcohol use are to be praised for counteracting the stereotypical behaviors which are still seen too often on regular programming.

Living Spaces

Many people, particularly children, are overly influenced in the standards and expectations they have for their own living spaces by what they see on TV every day. Screen living rooms have one thing in common: They're designed by professionals to be as pleasing to the viewer as possible, while never requiring upkeep. These sets are *not* homes—no one lives in these rooms! The expectation that these unrealistic settings create are often the breeding grounds for disappointment when a young viewer's real life doesn't measure up to TV's impossible standards.

Education

Although there are television characters who must have an education to accomplish what they do, their educational processes and achievements are given short shrift. Television all too often dismisses the educated person as a "brain" or a "nerd." Learning itself is often seen as a joke. For instance, on Channel One's classroom broadcast, in a series of commercials for the candy Skittles, there is an "interruption" of the ads as a voice-over booms: "We interrupt this class for a temporary emergency—for the next thirty seconds, think only fun thoughts." A series of "fun" thoughts follows, such as, "Students in many foreign countries go to school on Saturday and Sunday—suckers!"[6]

The portrayal of teachers on television has been labeled downright irresponsible by many experts. It has been a long-standing television tradition to portray teachers as incompetent buffoons, as in the programs *The Doby Gillis Show* and *The Simpsons.* The trend has become ever more insidious: A commercial for Coke shows a classroom of bored teens intentionally tuning the teacher out; a music video presents a teacher as a stripper; another music video shows male teens throwing a teacher through a basketball hoop.[7]

In fact, on most television programs, education is ignored or ridiculed, and the person seeking it is seen as weird. This is particularly true for the profession of scientist, arguably the most denigrated on television. Scientists are portrayed as older loners, likely to be foreign, involved in dangerous experiments, unable to maintain healthy relationships, often unpredictable, and very excitable.[8] Typically the screen portrayal is one of a mad scientist making destructive devices, rather than an intellectual scholar contributing to humanity's welfare. It comes as no surprise then that research indicates that children who watch a lot of television have a relatively negative view of science as an occupation.[9]

Health

Look at the characters on television and in the movies. Do you ever see them exercising? How often do you see them eating nutritious food? Yet the vast majority of them are fit and healthy-looking. We learn little from screens about how exercise and eating right play a substantial role in feeling good and staying healthy. The only people on TV who exercise are athletes. Television characters stay magically healthy without much effort.

Screen Images of Who We Are

Gender Portrayal

In 1975, a study of gender portrayal on television found that women on television are shown to be less competent than men. Rather, they are preoccupied with how the laundry gets done, how shiny the floors are, and how glamorous they look. Men, on the other hand, worked at diverse, interesting occupations and were the voice of authority on most commercials.[10] Two decades later, this dismal situation has not changed. In the *Dallas Morning News,* Manuel Mendoza recently stated, "That television is increasingly choosing to depict women broadly—pun intended—can be traced to a failure on the part of writers and producers to come up with scenarios that produce three-dimensional characters. Selling one-dimensional sexuality like candy, as an easy fix, seems to be the alternative."[11]

Keep count of characters in any television program and you will see that today, same as twenty-five years ago, there are still more male characters than female characters. In fact, seven out of ten characters on TV are male.[12] In video games, male figures predominate by a margin of thirteen to one.[13] The film industry isn't immune, either. Female actresses actively complain about the lack of good movie roles for women. In fact, this conspicuous absence of women on all types of screens has been referred to as the "symbolic annihilation of women."[14]

When they are present, females are frequently window dressing and do not play leadership roles in the action. Their hairstyles are more important than their career choices. Disproportionate numbers of bimbo blondes, cool babes, helpless victims, and damsels in distress act as role models for young girls.

Women are often seen as objects rather than as people. Their anatomies, or sexual parts, are constantly glorified. Even cartoon characters are subject to this degrading depiction: In the laser disk version of *Who Framed Roger Rabbit?*, a few frames show Jessica's nude body when her red gown flies up in the air.[15] Older children and teens are barraged not only with screen images degrading women, but with these same depictions in magazines and popular music. A scantily clad woman on her hands and knees licking a man's boot sells shoes; song lyrics with outrageous sexual references to women are commonplace.

And in recent years, an even more alarming trend has seeped into the mainstream media: brutality toward women, and women's sexuality being directly linked to violence. MTV is notorious for running videos with these types of images. But they are not alone. Here are some other typical examples:

A TV promo for the movie *The Three Musketeers*, produced by Disney, interspersed swordfight scenes with a woman's cleavage, connecting violence with a woman's body.

The video game *Metal and Lace: The Battle of the Robobabes* takes place in a seedy bar where players can watch "hot bod contests" designed to satisfy "most primal desires." The promotional material for this game features "hot, steamy action where female hard bodies fight to the finish. These strippers in armor pummel as well as peel."[16] This dehumanizing portrayal of women on screens takes place day in and day out in thousands of homes, theaters, and video arcades all across the country.

Men do not fare much better on the visual screen. They are depicted as all-powerful, all-knowing, and always in control, too often using violence and aggression to solve their problems — brutalizing beasts. Or they are portrayed in the opposite light, as total nerds, acting as ineffectual buffoons. Fred Hayward, the founder of the organization Men's Rights, studied hundreds of print and TV ads and concluded: "If there's a sleazy character in an ad, 100 percent of them are male. If there's an incompetent character, 100 percent of them are male."[17]

Stereotyped gender portrayals condition our children early on about sex roles. This is especially disturbing because children develop their gender identities at a very young age. It seems that television, print advertisments, and music lyrics want to display and exaggerate the differences between men and women. By constantly calling our children's attention to the dichotomy between the sexes rather than celebrating their diversity, gender stereotyping counteracts much of what parents are trying to teach their children.

One mother of two preschoolers described her frustration:

> To sit down and watch programs and commercials for children is to enter a time warp. There are ads for girls and there are ads for boys. There are cartoons for boys. There are cartoons for girls. Rarely, rarely, is there a toy commercial or a cartoon for both boys and girls. And these sex-specific images break down in the most hackneyed, sexual stereotypical way, making you think that you hadn't entered the 1970s, much less the 90s. Girls are shown nurturing a baby doll or making a woman doll more glamorous by applying lipstick, changing her hairstyle and her sexy clothes. Boys are shown using power and force through action figures and war toy machines. An aggressive mood is created by constantly repeating such words as defeat, destruct, terminate, battle, harm. I have both a son and a daughter whom I'm trying to raise as bias-free as possible. TV programs and commercials are definitely not supporting my efforts.

As their gender identity is being formed, American children and teens view an average of more than 14,000 sexual references and innuendos on television each year. Of these, less than 150 refer to the use of birth control.[18] In his book *Taming the Wild Tube: A Family's Guide to Television and Video,* Dr. Robert Schrag writes: "This rate of unprotected sex makes the dearth of pregnancies on television even more unlikely—but it is amazing how things work out when results are determined by script writers and not biology."[19]

Sally Steenland observes in "Growing Up in Prime Time: An Analysis of Adolescent Girls on Television": "By failing to provide even a rudimentary bridge between the two worlds—that of adolescents and adults—television misses their continuity and ignores some of the most important aspects of growing up.... Television has an obligation to paint a more realistic picture of the journey to adulthood and to provide role-models which teenage viewers can link to their own lives."[20]

Aging

Older Americans, the fastest growing segment of the population in the United States, are almost utterly missing from screens. Only 3 percent of all television characters are over the age of sixty-five.[21] This is not too surprising when one considers that the industry aims to please the young most of the time. In fact, viewers aged forty-nine and older are "unwanted baggage." This is based on statements from many television executives who attended the 1994 summer meeting of the Television Critics Association.[22] Viewers between the ages of eighteen and thirty-four are the core target group. This is true despite the fact that the highest income levels in America are enjoyed by people aged forty-nine through fifty-four. These are the folks with buying power. Yet networks pander to the young for two basic reasons: younger viewers are likely to try a new network, a new program, and a new product; and programs featuring youth-oriented subjects command higher prices in syndicated reruns.[23]

When older people are portrayed on television, the depictions are often neither positive nor realistic. For instance, older characters are more likely to be portrayed as doddering, forgetful, or victims of crime. In a study conducted by the Annenberg School for Communication, it was found that three out of ten senior citizens on TV were robbed or beaten. True statistics reveal that less than 1 percent of the elderly are victims of serious crimes.[24]

Older women, particularly, are badly misrepresented. Too often they are portrayed as physically incapacitated, overly concerned about the effectiveness of their laxative or their denture cleaner. The television program *Golden Girls,* a long-term success, was the first show to depict older women a bit more realistically. Few shows continued in that vein. In fact, most women on television are in their twenties.[25]

Race and Culture

Loring Mandel, an Emmy Award–winning scriptwriter, thinks that all television writers have a story similar to this one: "I wrote a TV script and showed it to several story editors. One asked what else I wanted to write. I told him I wanted to write about the life of Leadbelly, a powerful Black folk musician. 'Wonderful,' he said. 'I love his music! We'll do it.' Then he said, 'Of course, we'll have to make him white.'"[26]

Even though this incident happened more than fifteen years ago, it's still undeniably true that the majority of successful, powerful, and influential characters on television are white. A census of TV characters does not match the real world.

Where are the Asian Americans? Where are the Native Americans? Where are the Hispanics? A recent report, "Distorted Reality: Hispanic Characters in TV Entertainment," revealed that the number of Latinos in prime-time network programs dropped from 3 percent in 1955 to 1 percent by the early 1990s. Yet Latinos make up an estimated 10 percent of the American population.[27] Some individuals within the TV industry do lament this untenable situation. Ted Turner, president and chairman of the Turner Broadcasting System, Inc., introduced a six-hour documentary, *The First Americans,* written by the Pulitzer Prize–winning Native American author N. Scott Momaday, by saying that neither the motion picture industry nor the television industry has treated the story of the American Indian "properly."[28]

The problem goes beyond the lack of representation of minorities on the screen. For even when they are seen, how are they portrayed? On MTV, for instance, Black males and females are depicted as being more sexually active than their white counterparts.[29] Images of dark-skinned characters on video games are often portrayed as aggressive and hateful. Sadly enough, the only consistent use of racial minorities a child sees on TV is as the villain in children's cartoons.[30]

A predominant stereotype for Black Americans is found in situational comedies. "What we have is a continuation of the old nature of TV of Blacks as clowns for the merriment of the larger culture," says Theodore Hemmingway, a professor of African American studies at Florida A&M University.[31] Although television has other successful program formulas, such as Westerns, space adventures, cop shows, and courtroom drama, no minority-cast show has been able to break out of the sitcom mold. "The only other pervasive image of black life on television is Black people involved with drugs or guns or both."[32] Commenting on the problem of racial stereotyping on television, John Schott, a professor of media studies at Carleton College in Minnesota, observes, "We're willing to stretch for the sake of comedy but not beyond that, and I think it reflects an unthinking racism in our culture. It reflects our national unwillingness to look thoughtfully at Black family life."[33]

People with Disabilities

Persons with physical disabilities are seldom shown on screens: They are the least represented group in the media. When they are, it is more than likely to be in a special TV program or a movie that focuses on the disability itself. Not often are we allowed to see situations where disabled people are viewed as an integral part of a larger story.

In an educational video for school-age children, *Don't Be a TV: Television Victim,* a physically challenged young girl asks, "What do people with disabilities have to teach us about patience and perseverance?"[34] Indeed, this segment of our society has much to teach. And our children would benefit greatly from seeing such people on the screen.

How Children and Teens Are Affected by Screen Stereotypes

Stereotypes Make the Abnormal Seem Normal

Conrad Kottak, in his landmark five-year, cross-cultural study of television viewing in the United States and in Brazil, found that cumulative television viewing in childhood was second only to education as a prime predictor of what people will believe as adults. He concluded that the television has joined such factors as gender, religion, and income as "a key indicator of what we think and what we do."[35] The images on that little screen in the corner of the family room have tremendous potential for shaping a child's world view. And if those images are stereotypical, what will children grow to believe about other people, especially people who are different from them?

Other studies have found that adults who spend a good deal of time watching screens are more apt to perceive the screen world as more real than the world itself. Experts have observed relationships between heavy television watching and distorted perceptions of reality.[36] If this is true for the adult population, it must particularly affect the impressionable minds of children. When children watch screens without adult supervision, they witness a great number of stereotypical portrayals, which are not explained to them. Too often they come to believe that this inaccurate, misleading information is true.

Screen stereotypes present an unrealistic social context in which to develop an objective world view. For example, Bruno Bettelheim observes that long-term exposure to screen stereotypes may give children the impression that people do not change over time. He points out: "Television characters go through life unchanged by their experiences. Major things happen to them, and in the next segment they're exactly the same person they were before."[37] The normal course of human growth and change is often missing on the screen.

Teens are also affected by one-dimensional screen characters. In fact, some of the most stereotypical attitudes and behaviors are found on television programs that are aimed at youthful audiences. MTV is, perhaps, the biggest offender. Studies have shown that MTV depicts males as more adventuresome, aggressive, and domineering; females as more affectionate, nurturing, dependent, and fearful. "Female music video characters are excluded from most white-collar professions, denigrated as sex objects or as second-class citizens in the working world or omitted from the workplace altogether. While music videos made by several recording artists have presented adolescents with more realistic and worthwhile female roles than on MTV, most music videos do not seem to do so."[38]

Teens' ideas about relationships, too, are often tainted by the abnormality they see on the screen. What is the young boy learning about his future role as a husband and father as he plays a constant stream of "might makes right" video games? What is the young girl learning about love and intimacy as she watches soap operas, which

Tune In to MTV and Pay Attention to Teen Lyrics

- Act interested and ask questions about their music. What about it do they like? Are any of the images or the lyrics disturbing to them?
- If you have questions about the appropriateness or the meaning of any lyric, don't hesitate to ask the sales personnel in a music store. Or take time to listen. Many stores now offer headphones for that purpose.
- Ask your teen about his favorite music groups. Can he characterize their music? Does he know the music's roots? Has he done any in-depth reading about the groups' history? Why does he like these groups above others?
- Help your child understand that much of today's popular music makes social commentary and uses a great deal of satire and metaphor. Watch MTV with your child and talk about the intent of the images. Explain the role of satire; evaluate the effectiveness of the social commentary.
- Ask your teen to think about how freedom of speech relates to the music lyrics she listens to. Use this as an opportunity to talk about censorship and related issues. You and your teen may want to read and discuss other people's points of view in newspaper editorials and magazine articles.
- Your child will certainly have distinct likes and dislikes. Find out what she truly dislikes. What qualities does she look for when she buys a CD or watches a music video?

studies have revealed to show thirty-five romantic encounters every hour?[39] "A lot of what I've learned about sex, I've learned from the soaps," says Jenny, a fourteen-year-old high school freshman who says she has yet to have intercourse but is no stranger to sex play. "The soaps are really romantic. The people just fall into each other's arms and it's beautiful. That's how I'd like sex to be for me."[40] What she is not learning is that relationships involve hard work and risks, yet offer many opportunities for personal growth.

Screen Stereotypes Skew Expectations of What Is Possible

Images we receive from outside sources are much more easily remembered than internally generated images. In fact, in any competition between the two, the media image usually supersedes our own image. "Moses is Charlton Heston, the Sundance Kid is Robert Redford."[41] When you read the words Scarlett O'Hara, what images run through your mind? Do you picture Vivien Leigh? Or scenes from the movie *Gone with the Wind?* More often than not, even if we've read the book first, it's the movie's images that remain in our heads and replay themselves over and over.

Screen images are easily remembered, yet those which children see repeatedly are usually different from what they see in their everyday lives: in their schools, in their communities, in their churches, in their *real* lives. Affluent lifestyles, problems so effortlessly remedied, people so perfect and beautiful.

Pavel Lewicki, a psychologist at the University of Tulsa, has conducted research on the nature of our unconscious mental processes. His experiments suggest that our feelings about how people should look and how things should be are rooted in unconscious assumptions drawn from our life experiences. Because these assumptions are unconscious, we cannot look at them critically. When these unconscious learnings are based on screen images, they are apt to skew our expectations about what is possible. "Two hundred years ago, we would at least have abstracted these unconscious assumptions from our experience of the real world we lived in. Our 'rules' for how people should look would've been abstracted from the way our neighbors looked. Today, our standards are as likely to be drawn from the unreal world of TV, where all the data has been jiggered—where the women are thin ... the houses are lavish, the cars never break down ... No wonder we don't measure up."[42]

Children fall prey in especially dangerous ways to the unreal expectations fostered on screens. If their lives don't live up to the images they've come to expect as normal, who is to blame? Too many kids begin to blame themselves for what they perceive to be shortcomings—"I'm not good or smart enough to deserve that"—and experience a resulting problem with self-worth and self-esteem. Many television programs aimed at children and teenagers reinforce sex-role stereotyping, contributing to skewed expectations about gender roles. Cross-sectional surveys of children, adolescents, and adults have generally shown that the heaviest television viewers are also the most likely to express sexist attitudes regarding "appropriate" occupations for men and women. In a study of eighth to tenth graders, Gross and Jeffries-Fox found that those who watched a good deal of TV were most likely to give sexist answers to questions about women's occupations, access to education, and preferences for home-making and child-rearing.[43]

There's a further problem with the unreal expectations that the media create. For the millions of children who live in poverty, both in this country and abroad, holding a virtually unattainable lifestyle as the norm creates a hopelessness that may be contributing to the growing angst among today's youth. David L. Evans, a senior admissions officer at Harvard University, is worried that television's false portrayals of what is feasible harm his race: "This powerful medium has made the glamour of millionaire boxers, ballplayers, musicians, and comedians appear so close, so tangible, that to naive young Afro-American boys, it seems only a dribble or dance step away. In the hot glare of such surrealism, schoolwork and prudent behavior can become irrelevant."[44]

Screen Stereotypes Reinforce Divisiveness

Schools are spending hundreds of thousands of dollars on much-needed multicultural programs. Typical television programming reinforces stereotypes and the differences between people, and these trite, racial messages give children and teens ideas that foster divisiveness rather than the value of diversity. How can our children learn to respect the differences among people and cultures when they spend more time watching stereotypical images than they do interacting with real, diverse people?

Programs that depict both minorities and whites in powerful positions, cooperating with one another, are rare. With the exception of the hour-long drama *In the Heat of the Night*, these "crossover programs" generally have not performed well in the ratings.[45] More often people of different races or people who have varying viewpoints are pitted against one another. A teacher expresses his concern: "Yes, I believe that television generates violence. But in addition to that I fear that it breeds something worse—hatred, whether it be between classes and races or whether it be between husband and wife. It seems as though television producers are looking for anything that will stir emotions and keep us separated, hating each other and hating ourselves."

A study by the Center for Psychological Studies in a Nuclear Age found that American children get their ideas about what makes an "enemy" from children's cartoons. Petra Hesse, the lead author of the study, states, "War starts in the minds of men and women. We have to form an image of the enemy before we go to war with him."[46] Cartoons usually portray the enemy as dark-skinned and they abound with such slurs as "Next to a toothache, there's nothing I hate more than a Rusky."[47] The study found that these cartoons promoted fear and hostility and fostered prejudices that can last a lifetime. Dr. John Mack, a psychologist at the center, said, "We need young people who know about enmity, about hatred—who recognize it in themselves and in their friends, but who are not victimized by it and therefore don't victimize others ... who are able to see models of adults involved in collaborations and working on social problems ... and that they see leaders who are not simply saying this country's friendly, that country's unfriendly, but seeing what the complex realities of each of these countries might be."[48] With some work and imagination, television producers could present positive images of people and nations rather than the bleakly divisive ones we currently see each day.

Screen Stereotypes Promote Lifelong Attitudes and Behaviors

Once established, stereotypes are very difficult to change, and they will likely have perpetual impact on a person's life. In reality, there are differences in people—in their physical appearances, their cultural backgrounds, their perceptions of the world. That's what makes ours such a rich society. To deny our children this diversity by allowing them to watch television programming that depicts only a narrow slice of life is to impoverish them. What's more, it is to risk the chance that children will almost imperceptibly begin to reflect the dangerous stereotypical images all too prevalent on screens today.

Many of us who grew up in the fifties still bear the images foisted on us as children. Ozzie and Harriet may have seemed innocuous, even at the time, but their show, and others like it, have left an entire generation of Americans with the clichéd expectations of what a family should be: working dad, at-home mom. In actuality, Harriet was a working mother who came to the set every day to do her job as an actress. Yet our remembrances and our longings are for the stereotypical mother and wife, the cookie baker, rather than the real wife and mother, the harried, tired woman coping with the simultaneous roles of making a living and raising a family.

While screen images can powerfully shape attitudes, research has shown that children tend to interpret television images in terms of what they already know or believe to be true. And what children know or believe changes as their social experience and understanding increase.[49] The benefits of watching programs that portray people realistically cannot be understimated. The PBS programs *Sesame Street, Mr. Rogers,* and *Reading Rainbow* have been pioneers in providing culturally diverse material; Nickelodeon and the Disney Channel are also doing a good job. This type of commendable programming, combined with media literacy information, increases our children's understanding of the world and gives them the priceless gift of a healthy respect for human differences.

Six Family Activities for Dealing Effectively with Screen Stereotypes

Activity 1: Occupational Hazards

Introduction: The purpose of this activity is to show children that the range of occupations represented on television is limited, and that the portrayals of the occupations are often stereotypical in nature.

Recommended age: Seven and older

Instructions: Using a chart similar to the one below, have your child record information as he watches TV programs or movies throughout the course of a week or so. When he's finished recording his observations, discuss what he has learned about how television portrays people at work.

Occupation	Age	Gender	Race
Physician	*35*	*Male*	*Black*
Secretary	*22*	*Female*	*White*

The following questions will help direct the discussion:

- What are the primary types of occupations? Blue collar or advanced-degree?
- If you were a young girl choosing a career and your only options were those careers for women represented on television, what might your choices be? What do you think about this?
- If you were a young boy choosing a career and your only options were those careers for men represented on television, what might your choices be? What do you think about this?
- What occupations do minorities have on screen? Are they the same occupations that white people have, or are they somehow different?
- What are men shown doing most often? What are women shown doing most often?
- Many Americans over the age of sixty-five are not retired, but are working. What kind of work do they do, according to television and the movies? Is the screen version realistic? Why or why not?
- Do children work when they're shown on television? Do they do any household chores, for instance? Or do they have any part-time jobs?

After you've finished the discussion, use the information on the chart and have your child make another list of possible nonstereotypical roles that are seldom seen on TV or in the movies. Let him stretch his imagination and put a wide variety of people in nonstereotypical occupations. Examples might include an elderly waiter, a woman motorcycle police officer, or a male daycare worker.

Activity 2: Rewriting the Roles

Introduction: In this activity, children not only examine screen stereotypes but also take an active role in creating more realistic portrayals of people.

Recommended age: Eight and older

Instructions: Choose programs your child likes to watch. Tell him to pay close attention to characters who display stereotypical behaviors or attitudes. For example, in any situation comedy, look at the role of the father. In what ways does that character resemble real-life fathers? Look also at the roles of any minorities on the show. How "real" are those characters? If you found the person in real life, would he or she be like the character shown on TV? Would they look different? Would they act or talk differently?

Have your child write a description of one or two stereotyped characters he finds on TV. Challenge him to use as many descriptive words as he can. Then have him rewrite the descriptions of the characters, changing them to make a "whole" and "unique" person. How will he alter the characters' behaviors and attitudes? Have him brainstorm a list of descriptive words and phrases that will more fully identify each character. After he has done this for a few characters, discuss what changes he made and why. Point out how the roles change when the stereotypical attitudes and behaviors are removed. Have him discuss how the program differs with the characters' new identities. You might also have your child draw pictures of his new characters engaged in real-life activities.

Activity 3: Who's Missing on TV?

Introduction: This activity will help your child figure out what television often leaves out.

Recommended age: Eight and older

Instructions: See if your child can find what's missing on television by keeping a tally sheet like the one on the following page. Have your child watch a variety of programs for a week and record the appropriate information about the TV characters. Encourage your child to watch a wide variety of programs over the course of the week.

Age:
Under 10 ____________________
11–20 ____________________
21–40 ____________________
40–60 ____________________
Over 60 ____________________

People's income:
High ____________________
Medium ____________________
Low ____________________

Different genders:
Female ____________________
Male ____________________

Race:
African American ____________________
American Indian ____________________
Asian ____________________
Caucasian ____________________
Hispanic ____________________

Religion: ____________________
____

People like you: ____________________
____

At the end of the week, discuss with your child what she has recorded on the chart. You may want to ask some of the following questions:

- Is there a wide variety of people represented on TV? If not, who is shown, and who is missing?
- Which are there more of, men or women?
- What ethnic group appears more often?

- Did you find any characters who resemble you? If so, what made them like you?
- Were most characters different from you? If so, in what ways?
- Why does television show stereotypical characters? What good does it do the television industry? How does it affect the viewing audience?
- What could the industry and the audience gain if more complex, fully developed characters were represented?

Activity 4: Charting and Discussing TV Stereotypes

Introduction: This activity can help children identify stereotypical roles, behaviors, and attitudes on programs and commercials they regularly watch. By recording their observations and discussing them with a caring adult, children can learn to recognize and interpret the prejudicial and insensitive portrayals they see on television.

Recommended age: Ten and older

Instructions: Pick a program that you and your family regularly watch. Instruct family members that as you watch the program together, each member will be looking for any stereotypical renditions of age, gender, and race. Each person should have paper and pencil to record their observations. At the end of the program, turn off the television and discuss everyone's observations. Using each family member's notes, compile a master list of the stereotypical statements and portrayals that were observed. This discussion can be made more interesting if you've taped the program, so you can refer back to it while you talk.

Activity 5: What Do Others Think about TV Stereotypes?

Introduction: This activity gives children a chance to talk with others about their reactions to stereotypical TV portrayals. Children will gain valuable communication skills through discussion and interviewing techniques; they'll also learn much about real-life reactions to TV-world messages, helping them to distinguish important differences between the two worlds.

Recommended age: Ten and older

Instructions: Before starting this activity, your child should complete the charting and discussion of TV stereotypes in Activity 4. To begin this activity, ask your child to share with you some questions he'd like to ask other people about TV stereotypes. Help him come up with some possible questions, such as:

- Do you think the TV portrayal of men, women, ethnic groups, and so on, could be improved? Why or why not?
- What group/s of people are missing most often from news programs? from family comedies? from children's cartoons? from cop shows? from MTV? from your favorite shows?
- What programs do you watch regularly that depict people in diverse roles? What do you like about these programs?
- Do you think commercials promote stereotypical images? If yes, can you think of some examples?
- How would you change television to promote character diversity?

After your child has come up with his questions, have him write them down. Next, have him identify whom he will talk with. A parent, grandparent, neighbor, or a family friend are a few possibilities. Help him set up a time with each when he can ask his questions and discuss them—twenty or thirty minutes would be adequate. Also, if it's all right with the interviewee, your child may want to bring a cassette recorder and tape the interview.

Throughout the course of a week or two, your child conducts the interviews. Encourage him to write down the interviewees' responses, but only if he is comfortable doing so. It's important here to stress the enjoyment of talking with someone, sharing ideas, and learning others' opinions. Keep the activity nonthreatening and at your child's ability level. After the interviews have been conducted, sit down with your child for a debriefing session:

- Were some people's reactions similar? different? Why do you think this is so?
- What were some of the shows mentioned that do a good job portraying diversity? Do you agree with these opinions? Why or why not? What other shows might you add?
- Do you think people's ideas for changing TV programs to include more diversity were reasonable? Why or why not?

- Did you learn any surprising information? What?
- Did you enjoy the activity? Why or why not? What did you learn from the entire process? Would you do it again? Why or why not?

Activity 6: Hollywood Heroes

Introduction: Movies that you and your children see either on television or at the theater often show men and women in unrealistic roles of heroism. The screen version of heroism is usually not the definition of heroism that we'd like our children to have. This activity will encourage your child to explore the stereotypes that Hollywood often attributes to some heroes, and to compare these portrayals with the definition of a true hero.

Recommended age: Eleven and older

Instructions: Below you'll find a list of descriptions that contain attributes of both Hollywood heroes and of true heroes. Have your child divide the list into two columns, the first headed with "Hollywood Heroes," the second headed with "True Heroes." Have your child think about the heroes she sees in the movies. Which descriptions most closely match a Hollywood hero? Which descriptions would fit a real-life hero?

Fighting somebody
Rescuing a cat from a tree
Driving recklessly
Helping an elderly person across the street
Talking through a problem to a workable solution
Rescuing a person from drowning
Having a bodybuilder's physique
Winning at all costs
Taking care of homeless people
Using fists or guns to solve problems
Knowing when and how to compromise
Taking somebody hostage
Coaching a kids' sports team
Behaving promiscuously
Volunteering in the community
Lying and cheating

After your child has compiled the two lists, have him read the characteristics to you for each type of hero. Here you might ask your child to add other descriptions for either type. Discuss the differences and the discrepancies between the two types. You might ask your child to define what a hero is. These topics might illuminate your discussion:

- In the last few movies you've seen, were the characters Hollywood types? Describe what the characters actually looked like. How did they fit the stereotype?
- Would it be possible to recast the Hollywood hero by incorporating some of the characteristics of the true hero? If that new hero starred in a new movie, would it be a movie you'd go to? Why or why not?
- Think of some people whom many would agree are true heroes—Mother Teresa, Martin Luther King. Which of their characteristics cause them to be considered heroes? How different are they from the typical Hollywood hero?
- List the three most important characteristics for a Hollywood hero and the three most important characteristics for a real hero. Do they have anything in common?
- Is your teacher a hero? Why or why not?
- Are your parents heroes? Why or why not?
- Do you know any heroes?
- How might you be able to meet a hero?
- Do you think that if you met Arnold Schwarzenegger at home, he'd act like he does in the movies? Does he solve his real-life problems with a gun?
- Is it necessary that heroes be perfect people? Why or why not?
- Would you like to be a hero? How might that happen?
- How has Hollywood stereotyped heroes? What effect does that have on the viewing audience?
- Has Hollywood's stereotyping affected our society's view of what makes a hero?

7

Family Media Literacy Activities

Children can enjoy becoming media literate. We have designed these additional activities with both family fun and learning in mind. Keep it light; concentrate on the beneficial and interesting aspects of the projects. Involve your child in choosing the activities. You may want to include your children's friends in the fun.

After the twenty-three general media literacy activities, you'll find activities that address the basic topics in this book—violence, advertising, news, and stereotypes. Activities are grouped for younger and older children.

General Media Literacy Activities

TV and books. Keep track of the dates when a TV version of a book is scheduled to air and encourage your kids to read the book first, or follow up the program by suggesting they read the book afterwards. Great discussions can result from comparing the original book and the TV version.

Use TV to expand children's interests. Link TV programs with your kids' interests, activities, and hobbies. A child interested in crafts can watch craft programs for encouragement and ideas; after viewing a wildlife show, take the kids to a zoo and have them recall what they learned about animals from the TV program.

Time capsule. Ask your child to imagine that he or she has been given the job of choosing five television programs that will be included in a time capsule, not to be opened for one hundred years.

Discuss what type of society these shows might reflect to a child opening the time capsule one hundred years from now.

Different viewpoints. All family members will watch one program together. The TV is then turned off and each person writes a few sentences about their opinions about the show. Discuss and compare everyone's opinions, pointing out to your child how different people will like or dislike the same program.

Watch a show being taped. Take kids to a television program taping either locally or as part of a family trip to New York or Los Angeles. To make the trip more meaningful, have your children draw the set, take notes on the format of the show, note the special effects, and talk about what it was like being in the audience. Is the audience important to the show? How?

A field trip. Take a field trip to a local TV station. Call ahead to make the arrangements; stations normally have hours and tours set up for the general public. If the show is taped during school hours, ask your child's teacher if an oral or written report for extra credit could be done by your child.

Make up an alternate title. When you're watching a TV program or movie with your child, ask him or her to exercise imagination and think of another title. To get things rolling, suggest an alternate title yourself.

Compare what you see with what you expect. With your child, come up with a description of a show before watching it, based on what you've read in a TV schedule. Predict how the characters will act and how the plot will unfold. When the program ends, take a few minutes to talk about what you saw: Did either of you notice any differences between what was written in the TV schedule and what was actually shown? Were either of you surprised by anything you saw? Is the show what you expected it would be? Why or why not?

Which category does it fit? Using a television guide, your child will list all the shows she or he watches, then divide them into the following categories: comedy, news, cartoons, sitcoms, dramas, soap operas, police shows, sporting events, educational programs, and documentaries. Which is her or his favorite category and show? Why?

Predict what will happen. During commercial breaks, ask your child to predict what will happen next in the program. You can discuss such questions as: If you were the scriptwriter, how would you end this story? What do you think the main characters will do next? Is it easy or difficult to guess the main event in this program? Why or why not?

The guessing game. Turn off the volume but leave the picture on. See if your child can guess what is happening. To extend this into a family game, have everyone pick a TV character and add their version of that character's words.

Letter writing. Encourage your child to write letters to TV stations, describing why s/he likes and dislikes certain programs. Emphasize that giving factual and specific information will be helpful.

Be a camera operator. Have your child experiment with a video camera to learn how it can manipulate a scene (omission—what it leaves out; selection—what it includes; close-up—what it emphasizes; long shot—what mood it establishes; length of shot—what's important and what's not).

Theme songs. Help your child identify the instruments and sound effects used in the theme songs of his favorite shows. Have him sing or play the music in the show and explain what the music is doing. Does it set a mood? How? Does it tell a story? How does it make him feel?

Sequence the plot: a game. To help your child understand logical sequencing, ask her to watch a TV show while you write down its main events, jotting each event on a separate card. At the completion of the program, shuffle the cards and ask your child to put them in the same order in which they appeared during the program. Discuss any lapses in logical sequence.

A time chart. Your child will keep a time chart for one week of all of her activities, including TV watching, movie watching, and playing video games. Compare the time spent on these activities and on other activities, such as playing, homework, organized sports, chores, hobbies, visiting friends, and listening to music. Which activities get the most time? The least? Do you or your child think the balance should be altered? Why or why not?

TV jobs. Suggest that your child watch a television program, and have paper and pencil on hand for the conclusion of the show in order to record all the job titles in the credits. Videotaping helps. With the completed list, ask your child to write next to each job title what he thinks that person does. Help your child determine whether any of these jobs sound like something he'd like to do. Why or why not?

Winning and losing. Tell your child to watch a sports program and list all the words that are used to describe winning and losing. Encourage a long list. You can make this into a friendly competition, if you like, with two or more children collecting words from several sports programs and then reading them aloud.

TV and radio. While watching TV coverage of a sports game, turn off the TV sound and have your child simultaneously listen to radio coverage. What does your child think about the radio coverage? about the TV coverage? What are the strengths of each? the weaknesses?

Quiz show comparison. Compare and contrast the wide variety of game and quiz shows with your child. You'll see shows that test knowledge, shows that are based on pure luck, and shows that are aimed specifically at children. Which are your child's favorites? Why?

TV lists. Assist your child in making lists of all television programs that involve hospitals, police stations, schools, and farms, and all television programs that contain imaginative elements, such as science fiction shows or cartoons.

Television vocabulary. Challenge your child to find out what the following TV terms mean, and report back to the family:

channel
station
network
NBC, CBS, ABC, PBS
rerun
repeat
special
format
audience participation
assembly required
serial
first of a two-parter
90 minutes
spinoff
show host
anchorwoman or anchorman
newscaster
sponsor
sold separately at participating dealers only

Critical viewing survey. Ask your child to watch one of his favorite programs with you. Afterwards, you will both fill out the following

Critical Viewing Survey

Program watched:
Characters (List three to five and describe briefly):
Setting (Time and place):
Problems/Conflicts:
Plot (List three to five events in order of occurrence):
Story theme:
Solution:
Logic (Did the story make sense? Would this have happened in real life?):
Rating of the show (from one to ten, with ten being the highest):

survey. Then compare your answers. Are they different? Why? Are there right or wrong answers, or is much of what was recorded open to individual interpretation?

Activities for Dealing Effectively with Screen Violence

Younger Children and Screen Violence

As both an antidote and an introduction to the hows and whys of screen violence for children under eight, the following topics can be addressed:

Talk about real-life consequences. If the screen violence were happening in real life, how would the victim feel? What is left out of media-manufactured violence? Compare what's on the screen to the consequences of what happens when someone gets hurt in the real world.

Violence is not the way to solve problems. Emphasize that hurting another person in any way or destroying property is wrong and won't solve a person's problems. Point out to your child that many of the violent cartoon characters never seem to solve their problems from episode to episode, and that to use violence is to act without thinking of the consequences. Tell your child it's powerful and smart to find peaceful, creative ways to solve problems with other human beings. Brainstorm appropriate ways to solve problems.

Anger is natural. Talk about the fact that we all get angry, that it's normal. It's what we do with our anger—how we cope with it and express it—that's important. When screen characters hurt people out of anger, it's because they have not learned how to deal with their anger. Your child could make a list of screen characters who know how to deal with their anger in positive ways.

Activities for Older Children and Teens

Plot line for older children and teens. Make a plot line of your favorite show. Write down the introduction; the problem; the search for the solution; the solution; and the ending. Discuss (or write about) the personality traits of the main characters. If the program contains violence, is the violence really necessary to the plot? Is it shown as a solution? Could there have been an equally effective ending without the violence?

Emotional violence. Keep a tally of the types of emotional violence in favorite shows, such as putdowns disguised as humor, verbal threats, or name calling. Discuss with family members how emotional violence harms a person and why it can lead to physical violence. How could script writers change emotionally laden statements to more positive, healthy ones?

Get specific. What type of violence is most predominant in your favorite shows, movies, or video games? Keep a record of how many of the following acts you view in a week: threat with weapon, unwanted sexual advances, rape, murder, slap or punch, fistfight, run over or hit by a car, knife wound, gun wound, property destroyed. What have you learned about screen violence?

Sensational or sensitive portrayal? When a violent act occurs on the screen, how can you tell if it's there simply to draw viewers' attention or if it's there because it's a necessary part of the action? Start looking for the difference. Watch how you react. Does the violence move you in any way to feel compassion? Is the violence more about human suffering and less about blood and gore? How was the violent act presented? Where was the camera? Are you right in there with the action or are you an observer? Are you the perpetrator or the victim? Do technical effects distance you from the suffering inflicted? How?

Picture a world without media violence. Imagine that violence was suddenly eradicated from all television, movies, and video games. What would take its place? What would you miss? What would the general population think about the eradication of media violence? Would no media violence have any effect on real-life violence?

Learning to See through Screen Advertising

Younger Children and Screen Advertising

Blind taste test. Show your child how she can test the claims of commercials. Have her do a blind taste test. It can be done with a wide range of foods such as three or four kinds of soda pop, spaghetti sauce, cereal, and so on. Are the products as great as the commercials claimed? Can she tell the difference between a generic brand and a famous one? Can she identify products by name? Do the commercials make products seem different than they really are? Why or why not? This is a fun activity to do with several children. Have a taste test party!

Draw pictures of a feeling. Suggest that your child draw a picture depicting how he feels after watching two different types of TV commercials. What are the differences between the pictures? Discuss your child's feelings about the different commercial messages.

Picture the buyer. Younger children can watch a commercial and then draw a picture of the type of person they think will buy the product. After discussing the child's picture, explain how various audience appeals are used in commercials to attract specific audiences.

Cartoon ads. While watching cartoons, your child can look for specific cartoon characters that appear in the commercials. Explain the differences between the commercial and the cartoon: In the commercial, the character sells a product; in the cartoon, the character entertains us. The next time she watches TV, have her report to you if she sees any cartoon characters selling products.

The toy connection. When visiting a toy store, you and your child can look for toys that have been advertised on TV or promoted by TV personalities. Point out to him how the toys advertised on TV initially seem more attractive than those he hasn't seen advertised.

Attention grabbers. Think of several products or services and have your child come up with a dramatic, funny, or unusual approach to a TV commercial that will grab the viewer. Discuss why these approaches are effective in attracting viewers' attention.

Grade a commercial. Children can give a grade to the commercials they see during one program or over the course of a week. Grading is based on how well the commercial succeeds at making your child want the product. Give an A for the best, F for the least effective. Have them tell you the reason they gave each particular grade. Explain the manipulative techniques that commercials use. Discuss which of those techniques are the most effective and why.

Find the real thing. Purchase a food item advertised on television. Children then list the main ingredients found on the package. Discuss why the commercial does not inform viewers about ingredients or give much specific information about the product. Explain that a person needs to buy it and read the packaging in order to find out what's in the product—the commercial doesn't provide this information.

Invent a character. Your child can pick a product, such as a favorite cereal, and create an imaginary character that can be used to sell the product. He could draw a picture or role-play the character. Or, using puppets, he can stage his own imaginative commercial.

Activities for Older Children and Teens

Commercial tally. How many commercials do you watch in a week? When you watch TV, mark an X on a piece of paper every time a commercial is shown. At the end of the week tally the results, multiply by four to find out how many commercials you watch in a month, multiply by twelve for how many commercials are watched in a year. How many commercials will you see by the time you turn twenty-one?

Cross-marketing. Watch a current blockbuster film and count the brand name products shown throughout the film. Visit a fast-food restaurant and see what TV or movie tie-ins you can find.

Predicting ads. Select a TV program to watch and see how well you can predict what commercials will be shown by making a list of your predictions before the program starts. As you watch, compare what commercials are actually shown with the ones on your list. How good a predictor were you?

Product slogans. Watch for TV product slogans, such as "The Pepsi Generation" and "Have You Driven a Ford Lately?" Then reproduce them. Artistic ability doesn't count! What emotions do you feel when you see particular slogans? What do you think about when you see them? Why did the ad agency choose those cartoon characters, that actor, those colors? Can you think of another slogan for this product?

Slogan game. With a group of friends, make a game by collecting and recording all the advertising slogans you can think of. Do it individually or in teams. Give each team a week of TV viewing to prepare. Have a small prize for the team that collects the most slogans. Vote on which slogan is thought to be best and discuss why.

Create a radio commercial. Listen to the radio to get some ideas for creating your own radio commercial. Make your ad for either a real product or one you make up. Think about which market your ad is aimed at. Record your ad on a cassette and play it for friends and family.

Create a TV commercial. Decide on a product or service to advertise. Choose actors, scenery, music, and dialogue to make a TV commercial designed to sell your product. Where would you place your ad? Who is your intended audience? Present the finished ad to your family for their reactions.

TV and radio ads. Commercials on TV and radio are made differently. Using the same product or service, list the ways the commercials are geared to each medium and how the approaches compare to each other.

Types of commercials. Find examples of these seven types of commercials:

Celebrity endorsements
Major musical productions
Real-life drama
Unique viewpoint (up high, down low, underwater)

Hidden camera, testimonials, interviews
Special effects (animation, high-tech)
Tabletop (food on counter or table)

Describe or write out a description of each. Choose your three favorites and explain the reasons you chose them.

Advertising record. Keep an advertising record for a week, collecting information under the following headings: 1) What advertised? 2) Type of ad 3) Length of ad 4) On what show? Do you see any patterns, any surprising results? Share what you find about television advertising with your family and friends.

Targeted audiences. Find five commercials that sell products to a specific targeted audience, such as teens, men, young women, and so on. Track which type of commercials are used most often for this specific target audience. Explain why you think that this particular type of commercial is being used. Identify why the commercial is successful for that particular audience.

Emotions vs. facts. Decide which types of commercials are appeals to the emotions and which are appeals to facts or logic. Can you find a few good examples of each on television?

Body language. Observe body language in commercials. Notice head position, hand gestures, and eye movement. How does body language affect how you feel about the product? What does it say about what is being advertised? How many examples can you find? How can a commercial send a different message if gestures and movements are changed? You could cut out postures and expressions from print advertisements (magazines and newspapers) and see if you can find those postures and expressions on television commercials. How important is body language on television for selling a product?

Which product, which show? List two products that might be advertised on each of these shows:

Basketball game
Daytime soap opera
Evening news

Cartoon show
Golf tournament
Kids' game show

Why is a product advertised during a specific show? Keep track to find advertisers' patterns.

Be an actor/actress. While watching a commercial, role-play an actor's movements. How does it feel to imitate particular positions and gestures? Does it feel normal or does it feel put on? Is it the type of body language used in everyday life? Make up different body movements and gestures for an actor in a commercial, act them out, and then discuss how this new body language might change the commercial message.

Public television ads. Design a commercial that would be aired during a program on a public broadcasting station. Think about the audience that is likely to be watching this program. Since there are no commercials on PBS, will you make your commercial different from network commercials? Why or why not? Explore the differences between public and private sources of funding for broadcasting.

Satire. Create a layout for an original TV commercial that spoofs a real commercial. It's fun making an exaggerated version of a familiar commercial. For example, for a vitamin commercial, you could show a weakling transformed into Mr. Universe by taking only one vitamin pill.

Commercials in other parts of the world. What kind of advertising is on TV in other areas of the United States and in other countries? Find out: There is a great deal of information available in any library. Make this a research project for school. How and why are foreign commercials different from what you see at home? Are the differences merely in the kinds of products and services being sold, or are different appeals made to foreign audiences? This is a great activity to do when you travel.

Public service ad. Write a thirty-second public service message for teenagers about drunk driving or drug use. Do you think it would be watched by teens? What techniques might be used to ensure that teens would watch it? Do you think public service announcements are effective? Why or why not? This is a good activity for a group of children. Submit the public service announcement idea to your local station and see what happens.

Thinking Smart about Screen News and Talk Shows

Younger Children

As we stated in Chapter Five, TV news and talk shows contain elements that may not be appropriate for young children. If your child is under the age of eight, you should view these programs with your child and discuss them afterwards.

Older Children and Teens

Put on a newscast. You and several friends put on a newscast, using a newspaper or neighborhood event as content. Assign all roles—director, producer, writers, anchors, weather reporter, sportscaster, camera people, sound director. Use a video camera and actually tape the show. Be sure to show off your work to your families, or to your classes at school.

Newsroom tour. Take a newsroom tour and interview key personnel. Call local stations to make arrangements.

Letter to news personality. Write a letter to a specific personality on a news broadcast. Ask questions or make comments. You might ask about how the person first became involved in TV news, and what it would take today to begin the same career. You might also ask if that personality thinks that TV news is appropriate viewing for children.

Story tally. Keep track, for a couple of days, of every story on a particular newscast. Decide whether each story is negative, neutral, or positive. What's the final count? What does this say about the kind of news that is being broadcast?

Targeted news audience. Make a list of all the products advertised during a news broadcast. Reviewing your list, what can you tell about the type of viewer the program's producers are hoping to attract?

A news documentary. Pick a topic and research, write, and videotape a documentary about a subject of interest. Use visuals and props, interviews, and on-the-scene taping. Show to family, friends, and school classes.

A news story. After watching the evening news, choose one story and rewrite it, filling in information you felt was lacking in the TV report. You may have to make up information from your imagination or find further information in a newspaper or magazine.

Mimic a news anchor. Listen to the precise pronunciation of TV anchors. Have a mimic session! Who sounds more like a news anchor? Audiotape yourself to see how you sound.

Variations on a story. Look at how a particular story is handled differently by different channels. Use videotaped shows to compare. What are the differences? What are the similarities?

What is news? Make a list of all the science and educational stories covered in a week on local or national news broadcasts. Are there many stories, or just a few? Why?

Reporter bias. Listen for bias or subjective words used in news—does this reveal how the reporter really feels about a story? See if you can guess what reporters' or anchors' opinions are by how they deliver the story.

Screens and print. Watch a story aired on the TV news and find the same story in a newspaper. How do they differ? Why? Does one or the other give you more information?

Edit the news. Be an editor. Tape two different news shows from the same day. Then watch both and make a list of all the stories covered in each newscast. Do they cover many of the same stories? Now, acting as the editor, reorder the stories for each news program in the way you feel they should appear. Why do you think the station did it their way? Why are you making the changes you are?

Which story is important? Rank all the news stories from one newscast on a scale of one to ten with one being most important and ten being least important. Are the stories you consider the most important getting the coverage they deserve? Why or why not? Compare these news items in terms of their importance with those on the front page of the local paper of the same day. Discuss the differences between the content and slant of a story on TV news with the same story in the newspaper.

Keep track of the importance of news topics based on the time allotted for each. Using a watch with a second hand, record how many seconds are devoted to the top stories of several news shows over a week's time. Is this enough time for thorough coverage? Why or why not? As a news director, what would you do differently?

Write a letter to a local or national news program and ask the news director how she or he selects stories for their broadcast. Write to several different types of programs, such as the nightly news, a morning news program, a PBS documentary, and a TV talk show. Compare your findings.

News around the world. Keep track of all the different names of foreign cities and countries as you watch TV news. On a world map, locate the places and mark them. If you don't know how to pronounce the names, look them up in a dictionary. After doing this for a few weeks, can you tell what parts of the world, if any, get more reporting than others? What are possible reasons for this?

National vs. local news. When watching a news program, identify it as a local or national show on the basis of its content. Is what's covered on local news different from what's covered on national news?

Where's the 'new' in TV news? Read a local morning newspaper and write down the title of each main story. Then watch a local TV evening news program and make a list of the stories covered in the broadcast. What stories in the newspaper were reported on the TV news? How many stories on the TV news were "new"? Can you draw any conclusions about where TV news gets many of its stories?

Public broadcast news. After you watch a Public Broadcasting Service news program and another network's news program, think about the differences between the two. What are some of the differences? Why are there differences? What accounts for them?

Talk-show subjects. Watch for one week and list all the topics covered by the talk shows. You don't need to view the entire show; you can learn what will be covered in the first few minutes. How many of the topics covered had to do with strange or abnormal human behavior? sex? crime? abuse?

Talk-show audiences. Observe how the audience acts during the filming of a talk show. Were they chosen for their special knowledge of that particular program's topic? Do you think they were "coached" to ask the right questions? Are they typical people? Who would volunteer to be part of such an audience? Would you?

Do talk shows help people? Discuss with your parents the reasons why talk shows are so popular and successful. What makes people want to watch them? Who is the audience? Talk-show hosts achieve star status and fame. Do you think these hosts deserve all this attention? Why or why not?

Ads on talk shows. Who advertises on talk shows? Can you tell from the ads who might be watching talk shows?

Talk-show format. While watching segments of the different talk shows (it helps to tape the shows), take notes and then write a description of each of the formats. How is each show organized? What is the order of the topics? Is there any improvisation, or do you think the entire show is rigidly scripted? Does any show seem to have more advertising than the others? Which has more special effects? Which relies more on the wackiness of the talk-show host? Which format do you like best? Which set do you like better? Why?

Talk-show hosts. Watch all the talk shows (again using a videocassette recorder) and take notes. Then write a one-paragraph description of each host: physical attributes, personality, style. Who is your favorite? Who is your least favorite? Why?

Make a talk show. Roles include the interviewer and the interviewee. Choose your role and personality. What types of questions will you ask? What do you think your audience wants to learn? Can the person being interviewed talk about what s/he wants to? Is it difficult to get the interviewee to talk? Does the interviewer ask good questions? Can the interviewer get the interviewee to talk about what the interviewer wants?

Straightening Out Screen Stereotypes

Younger Children

Not better, just different. Children are never too young to start learning the message that differences do not make anyone better than anyone else. Point out how each family member has his or her own preferences, habits, ideas, and behaviors. Differences make us all unique and interesting. When your child sees a racist or sexist stereotype on the screen, explain that the writers of the script made an error in portraying the character in that light.

Change the picture. Play a game with your child: When she encounters a screen stereotype, ask her whether other types of people could play that role. For instance, if the secretary is a young woman, explain that men are secretaries, too, and that many older women are very competent secretaries.

Girls, boys, and toys. As you walk through a toy store, point out various toys to your child, asking each time whether the toy is made for a boy or a girl. Ask if the toy could just as well be played with by any child. Discuss the notion that toys may lead kids to think in sexist ways. Encourage your child to find toys that would be fun for girls *and* boys to play with. Then, when your child sees toy commercials on TV, point out whether only little boys or little girls are playing with the toys.

Older Children and Teens

Working people on TV. For one week, keep a list of men's and women's TV occupations. When it comes to work, how are the male and the female depicted—do patterns emerge? Are characters' occupations stereotyped?

Who isn't on TV? Make a list of possible nonstereotypical roles that you don't encounter on TV, such as a Hispanic doctor or an elderly policeman.

Inventory of roles. Over the course of one week, write down the minority group characters you see on television, including occupations and a few character traits. Compare and contrast these descriptions to the Caucasian characters on the same or similar programs.

Casting director. You are going to be the casting director for two TV shows. One will be a situation comedy about a neighborhood; the other will be a police show. Write a short description of the type of person you would choose for each of the following characters, detailing what they'd look like, what their personalities would be like, and how they'd act. For the situation comedy, create a postal worker, a neighborhood child, a sanitation worker, a house painter, an owner of the largest house on the block, a renter, two neighbors, the bad kid on the block, and the friendliest person on the block. For the police show, create a police chief, a sergeant, a detective, a secretary, three prisoners, and a janitor. Look over your list when you are finished.

Do you notice any stereotypes in the way you have cast these characters?

Sexism in advertising. Make a list of products advertised by women and products advertised by men on television. What do you see? Is there stereotyping?

Repetitive roles. Discuss the setting of TV commercials. Where are the women usually seen? men? minorities? older people? children? the disabled?

I know that person! Compare a TV character to someone you know who's about the same age in real life. How are they the same? What differences do you find? How "real" is the TV character?

Debate your parent. Here's your chance to show off your knowledge about the media. The topic of the debate is "Gender stereotypes on TV and in the movies do (or do not) influence teen behavior toward the opposite sex." Develop at least ten pro or con arguments for this proposal. Challenge your parent(s) to take the opposite view and present the debate at a family gathering. You may also want to discuss this issue with friends or ask your social studies teacher if a debate can be set up in the classroom.

Secret wishes. Who is to know if you secretly want hair like Cindy Crawford or muscles like Arnold Schwarzenegger? Think of how images of the ideal may have you longing for an image rather than valuing the individualistic person you are. When you watch TV and start having a secret wish, talk about it with your parents or a friend. See if they have any secret wishes, too. Discuss how screen portrayals can get in the way of accepting ourselves as we truly are.

Appendixes

Resources

Notes

Index

A

Reflecting on Media Literacy: A Checklist

There are many things to think about as you begin exploring family media literacy. The questions below will help you and your family reflect on some of the essential issues and focus your efforts. Use these questions however you see fit; remember, there are no complete "rights," nor any complete "wrongs." You decide what is best for your family.

- ❑ Do you turn on the TV as soon as you come home from work?
- ❑ Do you have the TV on as background noise for hours at a time?
- ❑ Does your family regularly eat dinner while watching television?
- ❑ Do you or any members of your family feel lonely without the TV on?
- ❑ Is renting and watching videos the only weekend family entertainment habit?
- ❑ Do you keep the TV on when friends come over to visit?
- ❑ How regularly do you talk to your kids about what they're watching?
- ❑ Do you point out inappropriate programming to your children and explain why it's not right for them?
- ❑ Do you limit TV time and content for your children?
- ❑ Does your family regularly discuss favorite programs, movies, and video games?
- ❑ When your child goes to a friend's house, do you know what s/he will be watching?

- ❏ How often does your family rent educational videos from the local library?
- ❏ Do you show videos to your children about topics they are studying in school?
- ❏ Do your children regularly ask questions about TV programs or movies?
- ❏ Do you preview movies before letting your children see them?
- ❏ Does the owner of your local video store know not to let your children check out R-rated videos?
- ❏ Does your child know how to use equipment such as an audiocassette player, a camera, a camcorder, multimedia software on the computer?
- ❏ How often does your family enjoy an evening watching little or no TV?
- ❏ How often do you talk to your child about the intent of the commercials s/he watches?
- ❏ How often do you talk to your child about media violence?
- ❏ When watching television with your child, how often do you point out how special effects—camera angles, lighting, and background music—impact programs and commercial messages?
- ❏ As a family, do you feel you have enough time for regular, fun activities together?
- ❏ Does your child enjoy playing nonviolent video games that require thinking and problem solving?
- ❏ As a family, do you choose what you are going to watch at the beginning of the week and stick to the plan?

B

Questions Parents Commonly Ask

Q. *I watched a lot of TV as a kid, and I turned out all right. Why so much concern about kids watching TV today?*

A. Even though many adults have watched a lot of TV as children, the time they spent in front of the screen doesn't compare with the time youngsters spend today—on average five hours daily. Also, children are beginning to watch TV at a younger age, developing the habit as young as three years old. In addition, video games and video movies fill the time that used to be filled by reading, creative play, and other developmentally appropriate activities. The content of TV has progressively grown more violent, and most children today watch more adult shows than they do children's shows. These changes over the past years are cause for grave concern.

Q. *How much TV is too much TV for my child?*

A. The American Academy of Pediatrics suggests limiting children's television watching to two hours per day. From our research, this may still be too much time for preschoolers. For most older children and teens, this may be an appropriate amount of time. However, you can tell what amount of time is too much for your child by considering the questions: Is my child's life balanced? Does s/he participate in a variety of activities? Is s/he developing the skills important for his/her age level? Is TV just one of many influences in his/her life?

Q. *When my child is begging to watch a show that I don't want him to watch, what do I say?*

A. Set the ground rules first. Remember, you have the right of refusal until your child is a certain age. Make sure that your child understands that s/he won't get to see everything desired. For young children, a "No" and a suggested alternative program or activity are usually enough. For elementary-schoolers, it helps to include them in the planning of what will be watched, so that they know a few days ahead of time what is off-limits. Explaining the reasons why you feel this show is inappropriate can be effective for some children. With teens you may have to resort to a flat "No" with some explanation as to why the show is offensive. Engage your teen in a discussion of the values you want him/her to learn from what is watched on the screen and why you can't support certain programs. Offer an alternative that you both can agree on.

Q. *I'm feeling guilty about having allowed my kids to watch too much TV in the past. How can I deal with it?*

A. Much of the helpful information for parents about how screens affect children's development has not been readily available until quite recently. Resolve that from this moment on, you'll begin steering your kids toward media literacy. In a very real way, they'll start this journey with a wealth of examples they can pull from their past viewing, which will help when you start to involve them in learning the hows and whys of screens. In a short time your children will respond positively to any steps you take toward media literacy.

Q. *My preschooler likes to watch videos over and over again. She has seen* Aladdin *eighteen times. Is this all right?*

A. Adults are constantly amazed at young children's ability to watch or listen to the same video again and again, and yet again! It's natural. Repetition is the basis of learning for young children. There is a point of obsession, however. When you feel that your child is coming close to the edge, find another video that may contain similar elements to the one your child seems locked into. Deep-six *Aladdin* for a few weeks, even a few months. As an alternative, set her up with an audiotape containing a story with a similar theme. This is a good opportunity to set screen limits early on and to explain that she must live with those limits.

Q. *How can I control the amount of TV my kids watch when I can't drag my spouse away from the TV?*

A. This is perhaps one of the roughest media literacy problems a parent faces. It's tough to go it alone, and it's even tougher to try to educate the kids about media literacy when you think your spouse watches too much television.

It's important to know that though this may be difficult, it can still be done. Don't unduly alienate your spouse by constantly harping on his or her TV habit. Ask if s/he'd help out by assisting you when you ask questions when the family is watching together. Insist that there be times (at dinner, for example) when the TV is off. If your spouse is watching programs that are inappropriate for the kids, make sure the kids are not nearby—outside, perhaps, or in their rooms. Better yet, have your spouse watch the shows in a room that's made off-limits to the kids. Share with your spouse what the research says about the effects of TV and video on children today. Above all else, make sure that your spouse does not believe that your quest for media literacy is only an attack on his or her TV habit. Emphasize that this is something you're doing because you're convinced it's best for your kids.

Q. *All my twelve-year-old wants to watch are violent shows. Should I be worried? What can I do about it?*

A. First, watch your child's behavior. Does it seem to be affected by what s/he is watching? Violent images can narrow the child's perspective considerably, present inappropriate models for problem solving, and create a continual need for more violence. Take direct action by setting firm boundaries about what TV and movies are appropriate to watch, and what video games you are willing to let your child play. Make a list of these, and post them prominently so your child is constantly reminded of the limits. In addition, it would be helpful to talk to your child about the violent images s/he has seen. Find out just how your child is interpreting these images. Explain that manufactured horror does not have the same effects as real-life violence. Don't be too hard on yourself for what your child has seen in the past. With discussion and consistent limit-setting, your child will emerge from the obsession with violence, and be able to choose a wide variety of television programs, movies, and video games.

Q. *How can I discourage my nine-year-old son from spending so much time playing video games?*

A. After you've decided how much time he *can* spend with video games, place a timer next to him as he plays. When the timer goes off, he must quit playing or he loses his chance to play at all the next day. Over the course of several weeks, gradually decrease the amount of time you've allotted. You may want to set a rule that he can't begin playing until his homework is done, his room is cleaned, his chores have been accomplished, he's participated in some physical activity, and so on. Make sure that his life is balanced, with plenty of developmentally appropriate activities. Remain resolved. Expect tantrums! And remember that the more he protests, the more he reveals that he's become addicted to these video games.

Q. *My younger children will talk about a TV program or a movie willingly. But my teenager isn't cooperating with the family media literacy discussions. What can I do?*

A. Some people need time to gather their thoughts after watching a visually provocative program or movie. You may want to try setting a time several days later for a family discussion, perhaps over dinner. S/he can focus ideas by writing a summary of what was seen, and what the initial reactions were, right after viewing. Give your teenager credit for being more mature than the younger children, and incorporate him or her into decisions made on how the discussion will be conducted, where it will take place, how long it will last, and how many questions each family member will answer. Don't make everything that your teenager watches a topic for discussion; this makes it seem like a burden. Make family media literacy discussions a regular habit and provide logical consequences for your teenager if s/he refuses to participate.

C

Sample Letters Children Can Write

These sample letters are examples of what children might write to networks and television stations.

2457 Highline Rd.
Showville, WA 98126
(206) 554-6948

January 1, 1995

Robert Iger, President
ABC Entertainment
2040 Avenue of the Stars
Los Angeles, CA 90067

Dear Mr. Iger:

I am a fan of your show *Blossom*. I want to write to tell you that I watch it regularly, and enjoy it. However, I do think that it should be on earlier, as my parents don't want me to stay up so late. Since the show is made for kids my age, I think it would be better if it could be on earlier for us. Is this possible?

❑ ❑ ❑

8340 Rose Blvd.
Anywhere, USA 10000

News Director
KURV
1212 Power St.
Albertsville, NY 12111

Dear News Director:

I am a twelve-year-old boy who watches your show sometimes. I want to tell you that I don't like the amount of violence you show on your newscasts. There are many important things that happen every day that aren't violent. Why don't you show some of those things?

❑ ❑ ❑

175 Allerton Rd.
Purchase, NY 10577

PBS
1320 Braddock Pl.
Alexandria, VA 22314

To Whom It May Concern:

I am a junior high student who has a question. My friends and I have a bet. They say you now show commercials; I say you don't. Who's right? I think you have sponsors, but they just mention their names and don't try to sell anything.

If I am right, please send me your policy about commercials. I want to use it in a report I am writing for school.

Thank you very much.

❑ ❑ ❑

Where to Write

Regulatory Agency

Federal Communications Commission
Mass Media Complaints
Edith Wise, Chief of Complaints
1919 M St. NW
Washington, D.C. 20554

Television Programming

ABC Entertainment
2040 Avenue of the Stars
Los Angeles, CA 90067
1-800-213-6222

CBS Audience Services
51 W 52nd St.
New York, NY 10019
(212) 975-4321

Discovery Channel
7700 Wisconsin Ave., Ste. 700
Bethesda, MD 20814
(301) 986-0444

Disney Channel
3800 West Alameda Ave.
Burbank, CA 91505
(818) 569-7897

Fox Broadcast Studios
P.O. Box 900
Beverly Hills, CA 90213
(310) 277-2211

Home Box Office
1100 Sixth Ave.
New York, NY 10036
(212) 708-1600

NBC Entertainment
President
30 Rockefeller Plaza
New York, NY 10020

Nickelodeon
1515 Broadway
New York, NY 10036
(212) 258-7579

PBS
1320 Braddock Place
Alexandria, VA 22314
(703) 739-5000

TNT/Turner Network TV
1050 Techwood Drive NW
Atlanta, GA 30318
(404) 885-4538

Turner Broadcasting System
1 CNN Center
Box 105366
Atlanta, GA 30348-5366

Major Video Game Manufacturers

Nintendo of America, Inc.
Corporate Communication Manager
4820 150th Ave. NE
Redmond, WA 98052
(206) 882-2040

Philips Electronics
Philips CD1
Customer Service
100 E. 42nd St.
New York, NY 10017
(212) 850-5000

Sega of America
Consumer Services 240 D
Shoreline Drive
Redwood City, CA 94065
(415) 802-1338

3DO
Customer Service
600 Galveston Drive
Redwood City, CA 94063
(415) 261-3454

Major Film Studios

Columbia Pictures
Entertainment Company (SONY)
10202 West Washington Blvd.
Culver City, CA 90232
(310) 280-8000

MGM Communications Co.
2500 Broadway
Santa Monica, CA 90404-3061
(310) 449-3000

Paramount Communications, Inc.
15 Columbus Circle
New York, NY 10023
(212) 373-7000

The Samuel Goldwyn Company
10203 Santa Monica Blvd.
Los Angeles, CA 90037-6403
(310) 552-2255

Tri-Star Pictures
10202 West Washington Blvd.
Culver City, CA 90232
(310) 280-7700

Twentieth Century-Fox Film
10201 West Pico Blvd.
Los Angeles, CA 90035
(310) 369-2211

Universal Pictures
100 Universal City Plaza
Universal City, CA 91608
(818) 777-1000

The Walt Disney Company
500 South Buena Vista St.
Burbank, CA 91521
(818) 560-5151

Warner Brothers, Inc.
4000 Warner Blvd.
Burbank, CA 91522
(818) 954-6000

Resources: Books, Videos, Software, and Organizations

The following resources for parents, children, and teens are listed by chapter to make it easier to find specific topics. Also listed are national organizations that provide helpful information.

1. As Children Grow: Screen Influence

Books for Parents

Dancing in the Dark: Youth, Popular Culture and the Electronic Media
Quentin J. Schultze, Roy Anker, James Bratt, William Romanowski, John Worst, and Lambert Zuidervaart • William B. Eerdman's Publishing Company, 1991

Top scholars explain the symbiotic relationship between youth and the entertainment business, particularly music and films. An extremely well crafted book with compelling insights, including little-known information on the development and purposes of MTV. Highly recommended for parents of adolescents.

Endangered Minds: Why Our Children Don't Think and What to Do About It
Jane M. Healy • Touchstone, Simon and Schuster, paperback edition, 1991

A modern-day classic, this award-winning book examines in detail how children's thinking abilities are affected by overexposure to media. Healy combines scientific and educational research with common sense to explain the fundamental problems in the educational crisis and what parents and educators can do about them.

Getting Your Kids to Say "No" in the 90s When You Said "Yes" in the 60s: Survival Notes for Baby Boom Parents
Victor Strasburger, M.D. • Fireside, Simon and Schuster, 1993

Strasburger, Chief of the Division of Adolescent Medicine at the University of New Mexico, writes an excellent guidebook for parents of teens; included is a chapter on the ways that TV and other forms of media influence adolescent development.

How to Have Intelligent and Creative Conversations with Your Kids
Jane M. Healy • Doubleday, Second Edition, 1994

Healy discusses the importance of speech to children's brain growth and offers guidelines for family discussions. She also provides numerous enticing questions that parents can use as conversation-starters with their children. A delightful, easy-to-use book to enhance children's thinking and creativity.

Media, Sex, and the Adolescent
Bradley S. Greenberg, et al. • Hampton, 1993

A thorough examination of how the mass media influence teen attitudes, beliefs, and values. Provides practical information and suggestions for parents.

The New Read-Aloud Handbook
Jim Trelease • Penguin Books, Second Edition, 1991

There is perhaps no better book to help parents find ways to make reading enjoyable for and important to their children. Trelease writes in a completely understandable way and gives many diverse activities that parents can successfully use. Offers a treasury of quality literature, with more than 300 annotated titles to choose from.

Positive Parenting from A to Z
Karen Renshaw Joslin • Ballantine Books, 1994

A useful reference book that addresses issues parents face today. It offers simple, useful solutions as well as treatment of television and screens as a parenting issue. Topics are listed alphabetically for easy reference.

Raising Curious Kids
Nancy Sokol Green • Crown Trade Paperbacks, 1995

A family psychologist offers one hundred unique, open-ended activities for children that involve the use of common household items to promote experimentation, creativity, and decision-making. Questions that parents can ask kids are designed to enhance a child's approach to life.

School's Out! Resources for Your Child's Time, Afternoons, Weekends, Vacations
Joan Bergstrom • Ten Speed Press, 1990

This book provides hundreds of activities that children can do in their free time. It also offers parents practical ideas for establishing routines, organizing activities, and teaching the three R's—resourcefulness, responsibility, and reliability.

Setting Limits: How to Raise Responsible, Independent Children by Providing Reasonable Boundaries
Robert J. Mac Kenzie • Prima Publishing, 1993

Because this book serves as a guide for setting and enforcing rules for children of all ages, it can be useful to parents wishing to set limits on TV watching and video game playing. A step-by-step approach with many practical strategies, this book is highly readable and immediately useful.

Table Talk!: 365 Ways to Reclaim the Family Dinner Hour
Steve and Ruth Bennett • Bob Adams, Inc., 1994

A hand-sized book loaded with wonderful discussion starters. Each of the 365 ideas is formatted for easy review within a range of 22 categories, certain to capture the interests of both children and teens.

365 TV-Free Activities You Can Do with Your Child
Steve and Ruth Bennett • Bob Adams, Inc., 1991

A must for parents wanting to find creative activities alternative to TV watching. Many time-tested endeavors are included, such as setting up a lemonade sign, along with newer, innovative ideas, such as kitchen camping and math with breakfast cereals! This small book lists each activity on a separate page. Lots of potential for family fun.

Your Child's Growing Mind: A Guide to Learning and Brain Development from Birth to Adolescence
Jane M. Healy • Doubleday, Second Edition, 1994

Healy conveys the latest scientific information on early development and then explains how children develop language, memory, and the abilities for reading, writing, spelling, and mathematics. Based on the assumption that "understanding a child's brain and the way it develops is the key to understanding learning," this book is a blueprint for guiding children toward optimal development.

Parent Newsletter

Beyond TV
11160 Veirs Mill Rd., Number L 15, Suite 277, Wheaton, MD 20902, (301) 588-4001

Advertised as a "publication for parents (and others) to help them remain committed to their goals for television's use in their home," this newsletter provides parents with a rich source of ideas. It considers these questions: Why control TV watching? How can parents control it? What are the alternatives? —all in the context of child and adolescent development. (Cost: $25.00 yearly membership)

Tools for Parents

SurfWatch
1-800-458-6600

This device will block your computer's access to certain information sites on the Internet that are unsuitable for kids. (Cost: $49.95)

TimeSlot
(919) 829-3525

A small, slotted box that attaches to the TV and limits the number of hours (per day, week, or month) the TV is on. It also can block out certain viewing times entirely. The device is activated by a card resembling a credit card, which is zipped through the slot to turn the set on. Once the viewing time is used up, the TV won't turn on. (Cost: $99.95)

TV Allowance
Great Scott Trading Company • 2590 California Park Drive, #20, Box 3638, Chico, CA 95927, 1-800-256-8974

TV Allowance is an electronic device that plugs directly into the TV. Once locked, only the parent can unplug or bypass the unit. Up to four family members can get their own "accounts" and "access codes" to program the amount of television allowed per week. This device has received the National Parenting Center Seal of Approval and comes with a sixty-day, money-back offer. (Cost: $99.00)

TV Key
1-800-626-8876

Parents install this palm-sized, mechanical device where the antenna or cable line attaches to the TV, then use the key to either stop the signal or allow it through. (Cost: $29.95 plus $2.00 shipping)

VCR Guard
Made by Playskool Baby, available in stores nationwide

This key-operated gadget fits into the VCR tape slot and allows parents to stop kids from playing videos. (Cost: $2.99)

Books for Children

The Berenstain Bears and Too Much TV
Stan and Jan Berenstain • Random House, 1984

Concerned that the family is spending too much time in front of the television, Mama Bear decides that there will be no TV for a week. Ages three to eight.

The Day Our TV Broke Down
Betty Ren Wright • A lesson in creativity for children aged five to twelve.

Fix-It
David McPhail • Dutton, 1984

Emma becomes interested in reading when the TV set breaks down. Ages three to seven.

Good Books, Good Times!
Edited by Lee Bennett Hopkins • Harper and Row, 1990

This delightful book is a compilation of poems about reading that were written for children aged five to ten. A great read-aloud to entice children to do more reading on their own.

The Wretched Stone
Chris Van Allsburg • Houghton Mifflin, 1991

This visual treat serves up an eerie tale about the wreck of the *Rita Anne.* Something is wrong with the crew: All day long they stare at a glowing rock that they have brought on board. A could-be allegory about the hazards of passive TV viewing, this book is a great choice for a family read-aloud to spur much thinking and discussion. Ages five to sixteen.

You Can't Sell Your Brother at the Garage Sale! The Kids' Book of Values
Beth Brainard • A Dell Trade Paperback, 1992

Designed with a format of appealing illustrations and easy-to-read print, this flip book covers such topics as self-respect, becoming responsible, cooperating with family members, fighting prejudice, protecting the environment, and doing one's best. A fun, commonsense approach to important lessons.

Organizations

Children's Television Resource and Education Center
340 Townsend St., Suite 423, San Francisco, CA 94107, (415) 243-9943

The center helps parents, teachers, and other professionals deal with issues related to children and television through services and products that promote children's social development and academic success. Resources available include the *TV Monitor Newsletter* and a series of TV Breakouts, covering such topics as violence, advertising, and music videos ($10.00 plus shipping). An award-winning audio cassette series, The Adventures of Christina Valentine, centers on the story of a teen who looks to television for solutions to her problems ($15.95 plus shipping).

KIDSNET
6856 Eastern Ave. NW, Suite 208, Washington, D.C. 20012, (202) 291-1400 • America Online address: kidsnet@aol.com

This nonprofit clearing-house provides information on children's programming in all media, including print, television, and radio. Resources available via America Online include the KIDSNET monthly guide to children's programming in all media, the text to KIDSNET study guides for a wide variety of video programs, and listings of free educational videos.

National Association for the Education of Young Children
1834 Connecticut Ave. NW, Washington, D.C. 20009, 1-800-424-2460

Dedicated to the interests of children through the age of eight, the association has developed a statement on media violence along with resources related to early child development. Advocates for public policy on issues that affect young children.

National PTA
700 North Rush St., Chicago, IL 60611-2571

The National PTA has developed packets of information about television and children, available to members. The National PTA advocates compliance with the Children's Television Act of 1990 and sponsors media awareness workshops. Check with your local PTA for membership and resource information.

Yale University Family TV Research and Consultation Center
Psychology Department, Yale University, P.O. Box 208205, New Haven, CT 06520-8205, (203) 432-4565

Parents may order reprints of articles and books written by Dr. Dorothy Singer and Dr. Jerome Singer, eminent scholars and researchers in the field of television and children.

2. A New Approach to the Home Screen: Family Media Literacy

Books for Parents

Beyond TV: Activities for Using Video with Children
Martha Dewing • Santa Barbara, ABC-CLIO, 1992

Aimed primarily at teachers who want to make videos an integral part of the curriculum, this book is also highly useful for parents and children who want to explore the world of video production. Designed for beginners, the author includes many practical activities and suggestions for discussion. Includes a list of video titles, along with print resources and helpful organizations.

In the Absence of the Sacred: The Failure of Technology and the Survival of the Indian Nations
Jerry Mander • Sierra Club Books, 1991

Mander addresses the political and economic systems in which new technologies are embedded. Includes a provocative account of how visual technologies influence culture, along with a revealing history of how Native Americans and other indigenous peoples around the world suffer from technology-based consumerism.

The Parent's Guide: Use TV to Your Child's Advantage
Dorothy Singer, Jerome Singer, and Diana Zuckerman • Acropolis Books, Ltd., 1990 • Available from the Yale University Family TV Research and Consultation Center, (203) 432-4565

This book explains how to use television wisely with children and contains numerous family viewing activities, including ways to help children learn more about video production techniques.

Parents, Kids & Computers
Robin Raskin and Carol Ellison • Random House, 1992

An activity-based guide for family use of the computer for both entertainment and educational purposes. Includes a section on setting up a home computer environment.

The Smart Parent's Guide to Kids' TV
Milton Chen, Ph.D. • KQED Books, 1994 • Available from KQED Books and Tapes • 2601 Mariposa St., San Francisco, CA 94110

A TV programmer's view of children and television, this book offers parents practical information and guidelines for using the medium as a learning tool. Contains helpful examples of programs worth watching.

Taming the Wild Tube: A Family's Guide to Television and Video
Robert L. Schrag • The University of North Carolina Press, 1990

An overview of how television impacts children and adolescents, with an emphasis on parent interaction. Lively discussion of critical issues by a professor of communications. Provides reviews of more than one hundred children's videos.

Taming the Wild Tube: A Television for the Twenty-first Century: The Next Wave
Edited by Charles M. Firestone • The Aspen Institute, Publications Office, 1993 • P.O. Box 150, Queenstown, MD 21658, (410) 820-5326

An excellent forecast of television's future, this collection of essays by communication and media professionals covers such topics as HDTV technology, public interest in an electronic-based society, and the psychological impact of a 500-cable-channel culture.

TV—Becoming Unglued: A Guide to Help Children Develop Positive TV Habits
Addie Jurs • Robert Erdmann Publishing, 1992

A small, easily digested book that addresses the problems related to video consumption.

Winning Your Kids Back from the Media
Quentin Schultze • InterVarsity Press, 1994

Although this book is designed for Christian families, professor and scholar Quentin Schultze's down-to-earth examples and practical suggestions make it valuable for all parents. The author addresses the concern that visual technologies have too much control over children and teens and impact our ability to parent them well.

Magazines for Parents

Computer Life
Ziff-Davis • 1-800-843-7799

For the more sophisticated computer user, this magazine reprints discussions about cyberspace, features new and offbeat products, lists the twenty best CD-ROMs and provides cutting-edge information on computers.

Family PC
Walt Disney Company and Ziff-Davis • 1-800-413-9749

Borrowing the format and feel of Disney's successful *Family Fun* magazine, *Family PC* is geared to parents of children aged three through twelve. It suggests educational computer projects for families, providing readily usable information.

Home PC
CMP Publications • 1-800-829-0119

Includes articles on using computers with children and for family entertainment. With a focus on education and personal productivity, this magazine is designed for families who use computers for work, play, and learning.

Where to Look for Educational Software

For up-to-date reviews of children's software, try these publications:

Electronic Learning
1-800-544-2917; $19.95 per year for eight issues

Technology and Learning
1-800-543-4383; $12.00 per year for eight issues

T.H.E. Journal (Technological Horizons in Education Journal)
(714) 730-4011; $29.00 per year for eleven issues

Software Too Good to Miss

For Children

Bannermania
Broderbund

A program that allows youngsters to create banners for all occasions.

Creative Writer
Microsoft

A wide range of activities allows children to create stories, newsletters, reports, and even secret messages, with a variety of tools. Interesting questions help children overcome writer's block.

Fine Artist
Microsoft

Maggie and McZee guide children through the tools needed to draw, paint, or put together pictures and sounds to make their own multimedia projects. The clip art might be a distraction for children who want a finished product quickly.

Gizmos and Gadgets
The Learning Company

A wonderful way to learn basic science without even realizing that you're learning! Players build auto, air, and alternative energy vehicles by collecting all the parts needed as they solve science puzzles. Then they race their vehicles. If the results aren't satisfactory, the player can redesign and rebuild. Various levels of difficulty.

Kid Cad
Davidson

Budding architects design houses, farms, castles, and skyscrapers by simple processes such as placing clip art on a vacant lot or through planning a large apartment complex and designing each unit complete with furniture and appliances.

Kid Cuts
Broderbund

This program, recommended for children aged four to twelve, allows them to make masks, puppets, puzzles, greeting cards, animal figures, and paper dolls on the computer. Afterward they can print them, cut them out, decorate them, and use them in their creative play.

Kids Studio
CyberPuppy Software

A powerful and user-friendly story-making program. A true creative outlet, sophisticated enough to appeal even to parents.

Kid Works 2
Davidson

In this writing program, children can create a picture story, type out an original story, or compose a story with tiny picture icons instead of words. When they complete the story, they can print it out or use the program's Story Player and hear the computer read it.

Math Blaster
Davidson

Math exercises are presented in a fast-paced game format.

Millie's Math House
Edmark

A cow and her friends guide kids through six fun pre-math activity areas.

Oregon Trail
MECC

Kids are in charge of pioneer groups who are making the dangerous trip across the country to settle in the Northwest Territories. All aspects of the trip must be carefully planned by the player. While on the road, any number of situations are likely to occur, all of which teach decision-making and logic. Children love this game; they will play it over and over again.

The Playroom
Broderbund

Children explore a playroom that is owned by Pepper, an animated mouse. When children click on the Mixed-Up Toy in the toy box, they can create their own original toy.

Super Story Tree
Scholastic

Young authors can feel like film directors with this program that allows them to enhance a story with music, speech, and sound effects. The readers move the plot along its electronic pages and decide the outcome.

Thinkin' Things
Edmark

A variety of activities for youngsters to explore, such as Flying Spheres, in which they make patterns and musical beats by controlling the direction of bouncing balls.

For Older Children and Teens

Algebra Shop
Scholastic

For kids addicted to malls, here's a program to help them work on their algebra. Each of the ten shops in the computer-screen mall calls for a different mathematical skill. Lots of variation built in.

Blue Powder, Gray Smoke
Core Group

A simulation of three Civil War battles that challenge the historical knowledge and planning ability of players. One or two players. Various levels of difficulty. Players must consider weapon type and use, field supplies, morale, and tactics.

The Cruncher
Davidson

A student-oriented spreadsheet program with built-in graphics and sound.

In the Company of Whales
Discovery Enterprises

With magnificent photography and a wealth of information in the form of text articles, this multimedia program provides extensive coverage on the topic of whales. A roundtable discussion of four experts adds interest for the inquisitive learner.

Mavis Beacon Teaches Typing for Kids
Software Toolworks

Action and gamelike interface will help kids learn the essential keyboard skills.

Science Sleuth
Videodiscovery, Inc.

Six levels of difficulty captivate children's imaginations and challenge their thinking skills in these innovative, interactive mysteries. The *New York Times* gave this software high marks for the way it humorously teaches kids how to spot the irrelevant and to separate the hype from important information.

Sim2000
Broderbund

The ultimate simulation game requiring such high-level thought processes as predicting outcomes and evaluating situations. Other titles also highly recommended include Sim Ant, Sim City, and Sim Earth.

Time Navigator Leaps Back
MECC

Driving an on-screen "chronomobile," users travel through American history from 1790 to 1900. The student must navigate by selecting the correct clues, which can be artifacts, headlines, works of literature, or bits of dialogue. The program can be played competitively, or not.

Undersea Adventure
Knowledge Adventure

A CD-ROM multimedia software program that allows understanding of ecology, biology, marine life, and oceanography. Hunt for treasure; electronically dissect different undersea creatures.

The Way Things Work
Dorling Kindersley • Available from Signals Catalog, 1-800-669-9696

Based on the best-selling book of the same name, this CD-ROM multimedia masterpiece brings 200 inventions to life, from telescopes and telephones to lasers and light bulbs. Includes 280 sophisticated animations, one hour of audio, 1,000 illustrations, 70,000 words, and 1,500 screens and pop-up windows.

Who'll Save Abacaxi?
Focus Media

Political science in action. The user is a leader of a Third World country, and will use knowledge of politics, economics, and international law to secure the future of the country.

World GeoGraph
MECC

This software makes it possible to visit 177 countries around the world! A unique way to study the world's peoples and cultures, it will satisfy simple curiosity. Provides a treasure trove of information for creating reports, graphs, and tables.

Zoyon Patrol
MECC

To capture the dangerous Zoyons and restore them to their natural habitat, the player must use maps, reports, and a database. This clever, multifaceted program demands sharp analytical, planning, and research abilities.

WEB Site Education Resources

The Cyberspace Middle School
(http://www.scri.fsu.edu/dennisl/CMS.html)

"It's not just a school; it's an adventure," reads the home page. Aimed at students in grades six through nine. It's not comprehensive, but it's growing by leaps and bounds. Also offered is a list of schools around the country with their own web sites.

Kids Web, a digital library for students
(http://www.npac.syr.edu/textbook/kidsweb)

A one-stop study site for students that allows entry to hundreds of resources in language, history, geology, sports, economics, and virtually all other school studies or activities.

Smithsonian Institution
(http://www.si.edu)

A myriad of resources offered by the Smithsonian's many museums. Both you and your child will be amazed at what is offered.

Westmont Hilltop World Cultures Hotlist
(http://westy.jtwn.k12.pa.us/mujr/WorldCultures.html)

A gateway to thousands of regional and national publications and newsletters around the world for kids interested in other cultures.

Books for Children

Fiction

The Bionic Bunny Show
Marc Tolon Brown • Atlantic–Little, Brown and Company, 1984

The reader learns all of the production efforts involved in creating the illusion of an ordinary rabbit that plays the part of a superhero rabbit. Ages five to eight.

The TV Kid
Betsy Beyars • Puffin Books, 1987

To escape failure, boredom, and loneliness, a ten-year-old boy plunges with all his imagination into the world of television. Events in his real life make him painfully aware of the costs of such an escape. Ages nine to twelve.

Nonfiction

Know the Score: Video Games in Your High-Tech World
Gloria Skurzynski • Bradbury Press, 1994

Amply and colorfully illustrated, this book provides an inside look at how video and computer games are produced, from the idea stage to the marketing stage. Kids will enjoy reading about all that goes into putting a video game on the market. The book can serve as a springboard for discussions about careers in video technology. Ages seven and up.

Lights, Camera, Action!
Gail Gibbons • Crowell, 1985

A step-by-step account of how a movie is made, including writing the script, casting, rehearsing, creating the scenery and costumes, editing the film, and attending the premiere. Ages seven to ten.

On Camera, the Story of a Child Actor
Joan Hewitt • Houghton Mifflin, 1987

Text and photographs present a close-up look at the life of the eight-year-old child actor Philip Waller as he goes to auditions, makes commercials, and films a television special. Ages seven to ten.

Printed Materials for Parents

Better Viewing
P.O. Box 538, Peterborough, NH 03458, 1-800-216-2225

This magazine serves as a listing guide for cable's quality programming and as a media awareness guide for parents: It provides many interesting articles by experts in media literacy. Offers family TV activities and and tips for parents. Published six times a year. (Subscription rate: $12.95 per year)

Video Librarian
P.O. Box 2725, Bremerton, WA 98310 • Published monthly eleven times a year (combined July–August issue), $35.00

Although school and public librarians are the primary audience, this newsletter can be helpful to parents looking for videos to support their children's school learning or who want to influence their local library's purchasing selections.

Videos for Parents

Choosing the Best in Children's Video: A Guide for Parents and Everyone Who Cares About Kids
A Joshua Greene Production, 1990 • Distributed by the American Library Association

This thirty-six-minute video, hosted by Christopher Reeve, features child development specialists, children's librarians, and children's video producers discussing what to look for in a quality video for children aged three to twelve. Examples from both fiction and nonfiction videos are interspersed throughout. A terrific video to watch and discuss with other parents. (Cost: $24.95)

On Television: Teach the Children
Mary Megee, 1992 • Distributed by California Newsreel • 149 Ninth St., San Francisco, CA 94103, (415) 621-6196

Narrated by Edwin Newman, this comprehensive documentary explores the impact of television on children and gives an interesting history lesson about the conditions of children's television in the United States over the last thirty years. Interweaving clips from cartoons, sitcoms, and music videos with comments by parents, teachers, and experts in the field, this video provides much food for thought.(Cost: $49.00 for parent groups and schools)

Television and Video: Children at Risk
Gloria DeGaetano, 1995 • Distributed by Train of Thought Consulting • P.O. Box 311, Redmond, WA 98073-0311

Designed for parents, this video outlines the basic ways in which the overuse of TV and video impacts children's development. Provides ten media literacy strategies to use at home. An accompanying booklet is provided for workshop leaders. (Cost: $24.95 plus shipping)

A Video for Older Children

Don't Be a TV: Television Victim
Media Watch • (408) 423-6355

"This is one of the most important videos to be produced this century," states Dr. Helen Caldicott, founding president of Physicians for Social Responsibility. Parents will find this seventeen-minute video a wonderful conversation-starter to help kids think critically about media violence, advertising, and gender stereotyping. (Cost: $40.00, individuals; $75.00, institutions)

Audio

The Adventures of Christina Valentine
The Children's Television Resource and Education Center • San Francisco, CA, (415) 243-9943

This award-winning audio series that teaches children about TV was aired on NPR. It relates the story of a young girl caught up in a series of strange events (she falls into her TV and meets even stranger characters) that ultimately lead to her understanding the nature of TV in a new light. Designed to keep kids' interest.

Sources: Books, Distributors, Collections, and Organizations

Resource Books

The Best Family Videos for the Discriminating Viewer
Quentin and Barbara Schultze • Northfield Publishing, 1994

Husband and wife, Quentin Schultze, a communications professor at Calvin College, and Barbara, a nurse, have teamed to create a selective list of videos. This book contains the "best movies on video," along with the MPAA ratings (only G, PG, and PG-13; no R-rated movies are listed), appropriate ages of viewers, plot summaries, directors and actors, and potentially offensive or upsetting material.

Great Videos for Kids: A Parent's Guide to Choosing the Best
Catherine Cella • Citadel Press, 1992

This book reviews and rates more than 450 children's videos. Categories include folk and fairy tales and tapes based on books, family topics, education, and music. Also included are lists of the bests: best detective stories, best videos encouraging nonviolence, best videos with positive female roles, best videos with creative problem solving, among others. Names, addresses, and phone numbers of 80 suppliers of children's programming make this a complete, highly practical guide.

Video Movies Worth Watching: A Guide for Teens
David Veerman • Baker Book House, 1992

Reviews written by individuals involved in youth ministries. Included are plot summaries, evaluations of quality, and suggestions for getting the most out of each film.

Distributors and Video Collections

Emerald Video Productions

150 Shoreline Highway, Bldg. E, Mill Valley, CA 94941, (415) 331-5185

In the Read to Me Series, a librarian reads timeless poems and stories from classics of children's literature, a treasure trove of ideas and visual treats for children of all ages.

Facets MultiMedia

1517 W. Fullerton Ave., Chicago, IL 60614, 1-800-331-6197

A catalog filled with classics. A great place to look for quality videos for both younger children and teens. Also sponsors the only annual international children's video festival.

Little School House Series

Home Media Entertainment, 5730 Buckingham Parkway, Culver City, CA 90230, 1-800-421-4509

For children aged three to five, this series provides an introduction to school readiness concepts such as shapes, numbers, and letters. For additional reinforcement of concepts presented, an activity book accompanies each videotape.

Miramar Productions

200 2nd Avenue W., Seattle, WA 98119-4204, 1-800-245-6472

This production company produces top-ranked, carefully created video and audio products for children, designed to engage the imagination and curiosity, while providing spectacular images which the whole family will enjoy.

Playhouse Video

A division of CBS/Fox Video, 1211 Avenue of the Americas, New York, NY 10036, 1-800-222-7369

Great dramatic entertainment for older children and adolescents. Also distributes Shelley Duvall's noted Faerie Tale Theatre Series, with highly imaginative scripts and excellent production quality for younger children.

Rabbit Ears Storybook Collection

Sony Video Software, 1700 Brooklyn, 16th Floor, New York, NY 10019, (212) 757-2990

Animation is leisurely paced, giving children time to reflect on the stories' plots. Classic stories and folktales are exquisitely presented. Audiotapes also available.

Tell Me Why: A Children's Educational Video Series

Tell Me Why, 730 Washington St., Marina Del Rey, CA 90202, (213) 821-3329

This award-winning, unique video encyclopedia is based on the book series by Arkady Leokum. Through provocative visuals and easy-to-understand dialogue, Tell Me Why answers children's questions about a variety of topics dealing with the natural sciences.

Traveloguer Collection
3301 W. Hampden Ave., Suite N, Englewood, CO 80110, (303) 781-0679

Not only for the world traveler, this collection opens up the beauty and majesty of different lands and people to older children and teens.

Organizations Distributing Information about Videos, Video Games, and Software

American Library Association
50 E. Huron St., Chicago, IL 60611, 1-800-545-2433

If you send $1.00 and a self-addressed, stamped envelope, the ALA will send you a list of recommended videos.

The Coalition for Quality Children's Videos
535 Cordova Rd., Suite 456, Sante Fe, NM 87501, (505) 989-8076

This nonprofit organization increases the visibility and availability of quality children's videos through a variety of means: the Kids First seal of approval is awarded to outstanding children's videos; the Kids First video display can be found at stores around the country; and a directory of high-quality children's tapes is available to members. (Membership fee: $25.00 yearly)

Digital Software Association
919 18th St. NW, Suite 210, Washington, D.C. 20006, (202) 833-4372
Gives computer software and video game recommendations.

Organizations Promoting Media Literacy

Center for Media Education
1511 K St. NW, Suite 518, Washington, D.C. 20005, (202) 628-2620 • Internet address: cme@access.digex.net

The Center for Media Education works with consumer and community groups to improve children's television and ensure compliance with the Children's Television Act of 1990. Resources include a community action kit, a 15-minute video introduction to the Children's Television Act of 1990, and the booklet *When Pulling the Plug Isn't Enough: A Parents' Guide to TV.*

Center for Media Literacy
1962 South Shenandoah St., Los Angeles, CA 90034, (310) 559-2944

The Center for Media Literacy is one of the best sources of information and curriculum materials available today to teachers and parents in the United States. Members receive a quarterly publication, discounts on books, videos, and workshop kits, and access to a telephone helpline. (Membership fee: $35.00 yearly)

Citizens for Media Literacy
34 Wall St., Suite 407, Asheville, NC 28801, (704) 255-0182

This nonprofit organization helps parents, teachers, and concerned citizens grapple with children's issues, First Amendment rights, and public access to media. Yearly membership ($25.00) includes subscription to the quarterly newsletter the *New Citizen.*

National Telemedia Council
120 East Wilson St., Madison, WI 53703, (608) 257-7712

The oldest national media literacy organization in the United States, NTC provides information and resources primarily for teachers. It also offers a workshop for parent groups called Media Literacy as a Life Skill: Managing Television in the Family. The annual $30.00 membership includes a subscription to *Telemedium, the Journal of Media Literacy.*

Strategies for Media Literacy
1095 Market St., Suite 617, San Francisco, CA 94103, (415) 621-2911
Internet address: ktyner@fwl.edu; bulletin board service (415) 621-5156

This organization is the first to have a media literacy electronic bulletin board to link like-minded individuals. They promote media literacy primarily through workshops for teachers, parents, and community groups and have a number of printed resources available, along with a videodisk on TV advertising.

3. Bam! Smash! Pow! Screen Violence

Books for Parents

Children and Violence
Eds. C. Chiland and J. G. Young • Jason Aronson, 1994

A collection of essays by experts in the field examines one of the most serious problems of our society. The essay "Television and the Development of the Superego," by Dr. Brandon Centerwall, offers a provocative read about the influence of media violence on children's identity.

Video Kids
Eugene F. Provenzo, Jr. • Harvard University Press, 1991

Provenzo explores the central point that "from a social and cultural point of view, video games are neither a neutral nor a trivial technology." With an interdisciplinary approach, drawing on educational and psychological literature, he covers such topics as the market and research, play and the cultural content of video games, aggression, and the portrayal of women. A must-read for parents dealing with young video-game enthusiasts.

Hollywood vs. America: Popular Culture and the War on Traditional Values
Michael Medved • HarperCollins, 1992

Michael Medved, a respected film critic and co-host of *Sneak Previews,* paints a grim picture of how feature films have contributed to "our cultural nuthouse." With explicit examples and articulate discussion, Medved argues that Hollywood is inflicting its values on American families. Includes a well-researched chapter on media violence.

Who's Calling the Shots? How to Respond Effectively to Children's Fascination with War Play and War Toys
Nancy Carlsson-Paige and Diane E. Levin • New Society Publishers, 1990

The authors, early childhood specialists, have designed a uniquely insightful book about war play and how the media age has altered it. Providing concrete steps for parents to guide young children's play in healthy directions, the book also contains invaluable information and resource lists.

Deadly Consequences: How Violence Is Destroying Our Teenage Population and a Plan to Begin Solving the Problem
Deborah Prothrow-Stith, M.D. • HarperCollins, 1991

A compelling overview of the problem of youth violence. Chapter Three, "Teaching Our Kids to Kill," provides an excellent summary of how media violence affects the developing teen.

Printed Materials for Parents

Beyond Blame: Challenging Violence in the Media
Center for Media Literacy • (310) 559-2944

An innovative and comprehensive community education program applying the principles of media literacy education to violence reduction and prevention. *Beyond Blame* contains lesson plans, ready-to-use handouts, and audio/video resources for all age groups. Different components are available for community groups, children, teens, and parents, or the complete package is available for $249.95.

Books for Children

Fighting the Invisible Enemy: Understanding the Effects of Conditioning and *Why Is Everybody Always Picking on Me: A Guide to Handling Bullies*
Terrence Webster-Doyle • Atrium Society Publications, 1992

These two books are part of the Education for Peace Series, written for children aged eight to fourteen. Both books help children understand how they become conditioned to violence. Provides concrete, specific strategies for cooperating with others and resolving conflict in peaceful ways.

Books for Teens

Voices from the Future: Our Children Tell Us about Violence in America
Edited by Susan Goodwillie, generated by Children's Express • Crown Publishers, 1993

In the introduction, the noted educator Jonathan Kozol explains this book's significance: "Here at last we have an oral history of poverty and violence in the United States in which the questions have been posed and answers given by young people. It is a shocking and compelling work, refreshing in the vividness of detail, terrifying in the narratives that fill its pages, ultimately redemptive in the visionary longings that so many of these fascinating children and teenagers have been able to express." An extremely valuable book for the entire family.

Organizations

Atrium Society
P.O. Box 816, Middlebury, VT 05753, 1-800-848-6021

Atrium Society concerns itself with fundamental issues that promote understanding and cooperation in human affairs. Its main purpose is to address the ways in which our society becomes conditioned to violence. Atrium Society publishes books for children as well as adults, including *Brave New Child: Education for the Twenty-first Century.*

Educators for Social Responsibility
23 Garden St., Cambridge, MA 02138, (617) 492-1764

Produces and distributes several detailed curriculum guides, videotapes, and a journal on peace education issues for children and adolescents. Sponsors conferences and provides speakers. Local chapters throughout the United States.

Mediascope
12711 Ventura Blvd., Suite 250, Studio City, CA 91604, (818) 508-2080

Mediascope, a nonprofit organization founded in 1992, promotes constructive depictions of social issues in the media, including film, television, music, and video games. Its activities include informational forums, publication of original research, and story, script, and policy consultations for the entertainment industry. Mediascope is also a clearing-house for a wide variety of research and printed materials on violence in the media.

Mothers Against Violence in America (MAVIA)
105 14th Ave. #2A, Seattle, WA 98122, (206) 323-2303, fax: (206) 323-2192

MAVIA, a national grassroots community volunteer organization, strives to reduce violence in our society. It encourages preventive investment in children before they are affected by violence and advocates policies that support a safer environment for all children. Their excellent handbook, *Speak Up: A How-To Guide for Making a Positive Change in the Media,* provides a comprehensive list of names and addresses of key print and screen media sources.

National Foundation to Improve Television (NFIT)
60 State St., Suite 3400, Boston, MA 02109, (617) 523-6353

This organization monitors TV violence and works to reduce it, focusing on the hours during which children will most likely be watching.

4. The Coin of the Realm: Screen Advertising

Books for Parents

Dictating Content: How Advertising Pressure Can Corrupt a Free Press
Ronald Collins • The Center for the Study of Commercialism, 1993

What products and services don't get advertised? Why? This groundbreaking study on advertiser censorship of the media addresses these questions and explains why the messages we don't get can be just as harmful as the ones we do get.

Kids as Customers: A Handbook of Marketing to Children
James U. McNeal • Lexington Books, 1992

As noted in the preface, "This book is about the market potential of children ages four to twelve, and marketers' responses to them." Designed as a marketing handbook for companies selling to that age group, it provides interesting facts and figures that reveal to what lengths the advertising industry will go to capture the child market. McNeal tells businesses how to cultivate today's children into loyal, long-term customers.

Marketing Channels: Infomercials and the Future of Televised Marketing
Craig R. Evans • Prentice Hall, 1994

With charts, checklists, and diagrams, this book aims to help companies market products successfully. For the average consumer, however, the information can be fascinating. Addresses the ways in which screen advertising strategies will change as the nature of television changes.

Marketing Madness: A Survival Guide for a Consumer Society
Michael F. Jacobson and Laurie Ann Mazur • The Center for the Study of Commercialism, 1995

The authors advocate that childhood should be an "ad-free zone," and they give many compelling reasons for parents to teach an awareness of mass advertising to their children. Contains useful information about the effects of advertising on children and families, including a section on how commercialism erodes parental authority. Highly recommended.

The Sponsored Life: Ads, TV, and American Culture
Leslie Savan • Temple University Press, 1994

The noted media critic Leslie Savan describes how advertising transforms personal experience and self-identity into "the sponsored life." She argues that "our notions of desirable behavior, our lust for novelty, even our vision of the perfect love affair or thrilling adventure adapt to the mass consciousness coaxed out by marketing." An insightful book for parents and adolescents to read and discuss with each other.

Books for Children

The Money Book and Bank
Tambourine Books, 1991

For young children, this combination of a book and a bank provides a hands-on introduction to money management. Included are tips about earning, budgeting, banking, spending, and saving. Lots of colorful graphics. The book is in the shape of a bank and has separate compartments for all coin denominations.

The Totally Awesome Money Book for Kids and Their Parents
Adriane G. Berg and Arthur Berg Bochner • Newmarket Press, 1993

Written by a mother and son team, this book covers a lot of ground. Older children and teens can learn about stocks, how to balance a checkbook, and the basics of financial planning for college. Written in a humorous style, this book is fun to read and full of important information. The graphics throughout make it especially appealing to kids.

Books for Teens

Caution, This May Be an Advertisement: A Teen Guide to Advertising
Kathlyn Gay • Franklin Watts, 1992

Written in clear, concise language, this guide will assist teens in understanding commercials, ads, and the advertising industry, and will ultimately help them become educated consumers. Fascinating facts, figures, and human interest stories have special appeal to a teen audience.

Drugs and the Media
Mary Price Lee and Richard S. Lee • The Rosen Publishing Group, Inc., 1994

A small book with big print and colorful illustrations. Older children will also find it readable and informative. The authors do an excellent job of providing relevant information in a down-to-earth style, while unearthing the power of the media and of advertising to sell drugs as a way of life. Part of the Drug Abuse Prevention Library.

Get a Life: Or the Awakening of Billy Bored
Citizens for Media Literacy, 1993, 34 Wall St., Suite 407, Asheville, NC 28801, (704) 255-0182

A comic book designed to teach teens about the impact of Whittle Communication's Channel One on life choices and behavior. (Cost: $1.00)

Magazines for Parents

AdBusters Quarterly
The Media Foundation • (604) 736-9401

Sometimes irreverent, yet always provocative, this magazine is filled with cutting edge ideas from society's best thinkers and critics of mass commercialism. A sixteen-page insert, "White Noise," teaches teens media awareness in their language. A must-read for those interested in activism regarding advertising exploitation. (Cost: $17.00 yearly)

Media and the Earth: Challenging the Consumer Culture
Center for Media Literacy, Issue #51 • (310) 559-2944

Excellent articles by foremost social critics on how the mass media drive the consumer culture, leading to environmental pollution. (Cost: $5.00)

Magazines for Children

Zillions: Consumer Reports for Kids
Box 51777, Boulder, CO 80321

Zillions is an award-winning bimonthly consumer magazine for children aged nine to fourteen. Feature articles provide meaningful exploration of the advertising industry. Regular departments teach kids ways to spot manipulation techniques and encourage young readers to test products and send the results to the magazine. (Cost: $16.00 for six issues)

Videos for Children

Buy Me That Too
Ambrose Video, 1290 Avenue of the Americas, Suite 2245, New York, NY 10104, 1-800-526-4663

A great survival guide to television advertising for children aged six to twelve. It was produced by Consumer's Union, which also produces *Consumer Reports* and *Zillions.* Revealing commercials' ploys through vivid examples, the video presents effective ways to watch and think about TV commercials, with an upbeat, positive approach. This video first aired on HBO and received much acclaim from national parent and teacher organizations.

Videos and Computer Software for Teens

Consumer Seduction: From Romance to Reality
Center for Media Literacy • (310) 559-2944

This 23-minute documentary explores the impact of tobacco and alcohol advertising on people's lives. A great discussion-starter with teens.

Critical Eye: Inside Advertising
Strategies for Media Literacy • (415) 621-2911

This interactive videodisk can help adolescents analyze different ad formats. Through a variety of relevant examples, it provides numerous ways to think critically about the influence of advertising. Engaging and thought-provoking. For use with a Macintosh computer and video player.

Pack of Lies
Sut Jhally • Foundation for Media Education • (413) 586-4170

This 35-minute video is an eye-opening account of just how far the tobacco industry will go to sell cigarettes. More than eighty examples from cigarette print ads are used, interspersed with information from medical research and from secret corporate documents from the tobacco industry.

Selling Addiction: A Workshop Kit on Tobacco and Alcohol Advertising
Center for Media Literacy • (310) 559-2944

Includes a dynamic 15-minute video analyzing typical commercial and advertising techniques and a 30-minute video exploring myths and claims behind cigarette and alcohol advertising. In addition, a discussion guide and relevant articles are supplied to provide ongoing analysis of the issues.

Organizations

Center for the Study of Commercialism
1875 Connecticut Ave. NW, Suite 300, Washington, D.C. 20009-5728, (202) 797-7080, fax: (202) 265-4954

The Center for the Study of Commercialism (CSC) was established in 1990 to research, publicize, and oppose the invasion of commercial interests in our society. It works to expose the culture of commercialism and to limit the influence of advertising. The CSC regularly releases reports and educational materials related to issues of commercialism. Members receive a quarterly newsletter and discounts on all publications. (Membership fee: $20.00 yearly)

Children's Advertising Review Unit of the Council of Better Business Bureaus
845 3rd Ave., New York, NY 10022, (212) 705-0123

This industry self-regulatory group investigates inappropriate ads on local stations, networks, or cable channels when people complain about them. When a complaint is registered, the group usually moves swiftly; most initial investigations are done within ten days.

The Media Foundation
1243 W. 7th Ave., Vancouver, BC V6H1B7, Canada, (604) 736-9401

This organization is dedicated to media literacy and to creating a freer, more accessible marketplace of ideas on television in the United States and Canada. It produces video clips of "idea ads" for people to present to their local stations. The foundation also boycotts magazines advertising cigarettes and sponsors other citizen activities to support one of their goals: "To invade commercial television with uncommercials . . . to create a new media culture with noncommercial heart and soul." *AdBusters Quarterly* costs $17.00 for one year's subscription.

UNPLUG
360 Grand Ave., P.O. Box 385, Oakland, CA 94610, 1-800-UNPLUG-1,
E-mail: peacenet,unplug@igc.org

UNPLUG is a national youth organization dedicated to commercial-free equal education. Opposed to commercial advertising in schools, the organization's coalition partners are well-respected leaders, who include Ralph Nader, Peggy Charren, the Media Foundation, and Jonathan Kozol. UNPLUG provides media literacy materials for parents, teachers, and youth, including a video, *Commercial Free Zone.*

5. The Show's the Thing! News and Talk Shows

Books for Parents

The Age of Missing Information
Bill McKibben • Random House, 1992

McKibben, the author of *The End of Nature,* theorizes that so few people are called to action on behalf of our dying planet because their main source of information is television. After watching television for a 24-hour period and then spending one week in the mountains, McKibben wrote this account of how TV provides a distorted and incomplete picture of our world: "[It] masks and drowns out the subtle and vital information contact the real world once provided."

Censored: The News That Didn't Make the News—And Why, The 1995 Project Censored Yearbook
Carl Jensen and Project Censored • Four Walls Eight Windows, 1995

Published annually since 1990, this report features the top 25 censored stories of the year, comments on those stories by the original authors, and gives brief synopses of each of the stories. *Censored* also contains a resource guide to alternative print and electronic media and a listing of alternative media organizations.

How to Watch TV News
Neil Postman and Steve Powers • Penguin, 1992

Postman, a communications professor and author, and Powers, a television journalist, have written an intelligent, readable book designed to help viewers understand the difference between what TV news says it delivers and what it actually delivers. Providing the reader with a thorough examination of television news, they conclude with eight commonsense guidelines. Also good for teens to read and discuss with parents.

Media Virus: Hidden Agendas in Popular Culture
Douglas Rushkoff • Ballantine Books, 1994

A provocative, witty, and at times sassy discussion of the subtle and intricate ways the popular media manipulate and can be manipulated—by those who know how they function. Thoughtfully examines various angles related to the messages that "our brave, new media" are carrying into culture.

Tainted Truth: The Manipulation of Fact in America
Cynthia Crossen • Simon and Schuster, 1994

An in-depth look at how information comes to be distorted, and how that distortion affects society. An interesting read for people who want provocative ideas about challenging societal issues.

Books for Teens

Image and Substance: The Media in U.S. Elections
Victoria Sherrow • The Millbrook Press, 1992

Written in a lively, easy-to-digest style, this book is aimed at students in grades nine to twelve who want to learn about the complex realities of the operation of the democratic process within a media-driven culture. Scattered throughout are black and white photos and political cartoons that emphasize some of the more important historical developments in the evolving relationship between media and politics.

Who's to Know?: Information, the Media, and Public Awareness
Ann Weiss • Houghton Mifflin, 1991

Putting the public's right to know in historical perspective, Weiss illustrates how business, advertising, special interest groups, politics, and the media shape and manipulate the news and information that Americans receive. Listed as one of the Best Books for Young Adults, 1991, by the American Library Association.

Printed Materials for Parents

News for the 90s: A Question of Values
Center for Media Literacy • (310) 559-2944

Fresh perspectives on how news is changing, what is missing, and how to spot bias and misinformation in news coverage. (Cost: $5.00)

Organizations

FAIR (Fairness and Accuracy in Reporting)
130 West 25th St., New York, NY 10001, (212) 633-6700

FAIR's goals are to educate the public about who owns the news media, to promote the representation and expression of all significant viewpoints on issues, and to promote popular activism on behalf of the first two goals. The journal *Extra!* is published eight times a year. (Subscription $30.00 annually)

6. Typecast: Screen Stereotypes

Books for Parents

All That She Can Be
Dr. Carl J. Eagle and Carol Colman • Simon and Schuster, 1993

A sensitive and understanding presentation of the challenges and struggles that confront young women today. Valuable ideas and approaches can help parents raise more confident and competent daughters.

Failing at Fairness: How America's Schools Cheat Girls
Myra and David Sadker • Scribners, 1994

A book devoted mostly to discussing the discrimination against girls in schools, it also explains how boys are shortchanged. The authors describe how the school system perpetuates unfair practices and what needs to be done about it by parents, teachers, and society at large.

How to Make the World a Better Place for Women in Five Minutes
Donna Jackson • Hyperion, 1992

Packed with information, this book provides tasks and solutions for females of all ages. It also may help parents prepare their daughters for challenges they will face in the future.

How to Tell the Difference: A Checklist for Evaluating Children's Books for Anti-Indian Bias
Beverly Slapin, Doris Seale, and Rosemary Gonzales • New Society Publishers, 1992

A valuable tool for ensuring that children's reading materials are bias-free.

Prejudice and Your Child
Kenneth B. Clark • Harper and Row, 1988

This now classic book is a definitive look at how prejudice influences children and what parents can do to raise bias-free children. Many of the concepts presented can be used when examining screen stereotypes.

Teaching Your Children Values
Linda and Richard Eyre • Simon and Schuster, 1993

The authors present a plan to help parents teach values such as honesty and self-discipline as protection against peer pressure and the demands of a consumer culture. Games, family activities, and exercises are included.

We Can All Get Along: 50 Steps You Can Take to Help End Racism
Clyde W. Ford • Dell Publishing, 1994

An inspiring, informative guide for understanding racism and taking concrete, practical steps to make our world a better place.

Where the Girls Are: Growing Up Female with the Mass Media
Susan J. Douglas • Time Books, 1994

A lively account of how females on the screen have influenced both men and women over the past few decades.

Books for Children

Crazy Lady
Jane Leslie Conley • HarperCollins, 1993

Is she the neighborhood crazy lady ... is he her crazy son? Or perhaps something entirely different? Follow as Vernon discovers the meaning of tolerance.

Land of Promise
T. L. Tedrow • Thomas Nelson, 1992

Laura and other inhabitants of Mansfield, Missouri, face the problem of racism and a clash of culture when Chinese immigrants want to settle in the pioneer community. Part of the Laura Ingalls Wilder series.

The Rag Coat
Lauren Mills • Little, Brown and Company, 1991

More than anything, Minna wants to go to school. But she needs a coat. The reaction of her new classmates punctures her confidence. Set in Appalachia, this is a sensitive book about differences and acceptance.

Shades of Grey
Carolyn Reeder • Avon, 1991

A Southern boy, orphaned in the Civil War, must go to live with his uncle, who opposed the war. He slowly comes to understand another point of view about beliefs he initially holds deep and strongly.

The Shadowman's Way
Paul Pitts • Avon, 1992

A withdrawn Navajo boy on a reservation and the new white boy in town come face to face with enmity not of their making. Friendship overcomes stereotypes and ignorance.

Stellaluna
Janell Cannon • Harcourt, Brace, 1993

A charming story about a young bat who loses her mother and is raised by birds. She grows up thinking she is a bird, and then must re-adjust to being a bat when she finds her mother. Wonderful parallels to "fitting in" for children.

Yang the Youngest
Lindsey Namioka • Dell, 1992

A Chinese immigrant boy, whose family expects him to follow in their footsteps and become a musician, prefers baseball. His American friend, expected by his own family to like baseball, would rather be playing the violin. This book works through many issues to a realistic conclusion.

Books for Teens

Coping with Sexism
Rhoda McFarland • Rosen Publishing Group, 1990

Examines sex-oriented discrimination at work, in the media, at school, and at play, and provides tips on how to deal with this issue. A book for young teens to read and discuss with caring adults.

Gangs
Renardo Barden • Rourke Corp., 1990

Discusses the phenomenon of gangs and such social problems as poverty, racism, and drugs.

Spreading Poison: A Book About Racism and Prejudice
John Langone • Little, Brown and Company, 1993

Discusses various racial and ethnic groups in the United States and examines the problems of religious and sexual discrimination. Written for teens.

Think About Racism
Linda Mizell • Walker, 1992

Discusses racism in America and how it has affected history, the law, and contemporary issues. Gives teens an excellent overview of the complexities involved.

A Newspaper by and for Teens

YO (Youth Outlook)
Pacific News Service, 450 Mission St., Rm. 506, San Francisco, CA 94105,
(415) 243-4364

A quarterly newspaper written by and about teens, *YO* is much more than a compilation of articles on social issues, personal narratives, and creative poems. A flyer about the newspaper states: "It is one of the few informal networks . . . where kids . . . can talk to one another about their lives." Highly recommended.

Videos for Children and Teens

The Famine Within
Direct Cinema Ltd., 1990

An excellent documentary investigating the contemporary obsession with body size and shape by many North American women. This video combines the testimony of women who have been influenced by mass media and the demands of consumerism with the views of leading experts.

Hallelujah
MGM/UA Home Video, 1993

This 1929 black and white musical depicts the life of a southern Black family according to racist stereotypes prevalent at the time. *Hallelujah* may help teens put screen stereotypes into an historical context.

Prejudice: Answering Children's Questions
MPI Home Video, 1992

Peter Jennings hosts an audience of American children from various cultural backgrounds and leads a discussion about prejudices based on race, sex, religion, and disability. A teacher and a scientist carry out experiments to further their understanding of the roots of prejudice. A professor and a community development director examine some of the influences that shape children's ideas about the world.

Slaying the Dragon
Modern Educational Video Network, 1992

Examines stereotypes in film and television used to portray Asian women. Uses film clips from the 1920s through the 1980s and features interviews with Asian American actresses and TV news women to illustrate racist and antifeminist attitudes.

Stand Up and Be Counted Reacting to Racism
Modern Educational Video Network, 1992

Presents two stories of young people and their families making a difference when a racist incident takes place in their communities.

Warning: The Media May Be Hazardous to Your Health
Media Watch • (408) 423-6355

A stunningly graphic and provocative video about the portrayal of men and women in the media and in printed materials. Examines how media violence can lead to real-life sexual violence against women.

What You Gonna Do About Hate?
Coronet MTI Film and Video • 1-800-777-8100

A youth-created educational video by City Kids that focuses on how a multicultural group of young people feel about hate and what they think should and can be done about it.

Who Killed Vincent Chin?
Modern Educational Video Network, 1992

This video on racism in working-class America focuses on the murder of Vincent Chin, a Chinese American, in a Detroit bar. It interweaves the murder plot with social concerns and questions about justice.

Women Seen on Television
Letting Go Foundation, Inc. • (503) 635-7511

This 11-minute video is an incisive examination of the stereotypical portrayal of women on TV. The accompanying discussion guide makes the tape an excellent vehicle for family conversations.

Organizations

Cultural Environmental Movement
P.O. Box 31847, Philadelphia, PA 19104, (215) 573-7099

Spearheaded by Dr. George Gerbner, professor emeritus at the Annenberg School for Communication at the University of Pennsylvania, this nonprofit coalition views mass-produced and policy-driven TV programs as the modern counterparts of the stories that parents and grandparents used to tell children. It works to end formula-driven homogenization of media content and to create a freer, fairer, and more diverse cultural environment and a broader-based participation in cultural decisions that shape the lives of children.

Family Choice TV
National Association for Family and Community Education
P.O. Box 835, Burlington, KY 41005, (606) 568-8333

The National Association for Family and Community Education is an organization of more than 300,000 grassroots volunteers with the mission to "help cultivate a society where families can grow and flourish." The Family Choice TV Project provides resource materials, workshops, and other activities for the community that bring awareness for viewing television with a critical eye. Their information provides parents with details on how to watch TV with children to make a real difference, especially in the areas of stereotypes and violence.

Media Watch
P.O. Box 618, Santa Cruz, CA 95061, (408) 423-6355

Founded by the former fashion model Ann Simonton, Media Watch is the most prominent activist organization working nationally to educate the general public about how women and children are victimized by the media. A quarterly newsletter, *Action Agenda,* published in collaboration with Media Action Alliance, provides provocative essays and up-to-date information about programs and products glorifying violence, racism, and sexism. Provided are printed postcards written and addressed to offending producers and/or advertisers so readers can simply sign their names and mail (yearly subscription: $10.00 for lower-income readers; $20.00 regularly).

Notes

Introduction: Raising Media-Literate Children

1. Quentin J. Schultze, *Winning Your Kids Back from the Media* (Downers Grove: InterVarsity Press, 1994), 42.
2. Conrad Phillip Kottak, *Prime-Time Society: An Anthropological Analysis of Television and Culture* (Belmont: Wadsworth Publishing Company, 1990), 3.
3. Thomas Lickona, M.D., *Raising Good Children: Helping Your Child Through the Stages of Moral Development* (New York: Bantam Books, 1983), 350.

1. As Children Grow: Screen Influence

1. Jane M. Healy, *Endangered Minds: Why Our Children Don't Think* (New York: Simon and Schuster, 1990), 168.
2. Gloria M. DeGaetano, *Television and the Lives of Our Children* (Redmond: Train of Thought Publishing, 1993), 2.
3. Ibid.
4. Healy, *Endangered Minds,* 208.
5. Marian Cleeves Diamond, "Plasticity of the Brain: Enrichment vs. Impoverishment," in *Television and the Preparation of the Mind for Learning: Critical Questions on the Effects of Television on the Developing Brains of Young Children,* eds. Cheryl Clark and Kara King (Vienna: Ellsworth Associates, Inc., 1992), 8–19.
6. Diane Ackerman, *A Natural History of the Senses* (New York: Vintage Books, 1991), 307.
7. Eve Merriam, *there is no rhyme for silver* (New York: Atheneum, 1962), 20.
8. Healy, *Endangered Minds,* 201.
9. Bruno Bettelheim, *A Good Enough Parent: A Book on Child-Rearing* (New York: Vintage Books, 1987), 177.
10. Joseph Franklin, *Television: The Black Death of the 1990's* (Chicago: McDougal, Littell, 1993), 48.

2. A New Approach to the Home Screen: Family Media Literacy

1. Jerry Mander, *In the Absence of the Sacred: The Failure of Technology and the Survival of the Indian Nations* (San Francisco: Sierra Club Books, 1991), 41.
2. Diedre Downs, "The Mind Age," *The State of New Mexico Media Education* (summer 1994): 2.
3. Center for Media Literacy press release (6 June 1994), 3.
4. "Educational Video Center, New York," *Clipboard: A Media Education Newsletter from Canada* 8 (summer 1994): 6–7.
5. Ibid., 5.
6. Ibid., 6.
7. Ibid., 1.
8. American Academy of Pediatrics, Committee on Communications, "Children, Adolescents, and Television," *Pediatrics* 85: 1,119–1,120.
9. Edward deBono in *Developing Minds: A Resource Book for Teaching Thinking,* ed. Arthur L. Costa (Alexandria: Association for Supervision and Curriculum Development, 1985), 203.
10. Jane M. Healy, "Visual Technology: Vacuous or Visionary?" *Holistic Education Review* (June 1993): 17.
11. D. T. Max, "The End of the Book?" *Atlantic Monthly* 274 (September 1994): 67.
12. Fred Moody, "Virtual Kids," *Seattle Weekly,* 23 March 1994, 9–10.

3. Bam! Smash! Pow! Screen Violence

1. John P. Murray, "The Developing Child in a Multimedia Society," in *Children and Television: Images in a Changing Sociocultural World,* eds. Gordon Berry and Joy Keiko Asamen (Newbury Park: Sage Publications, 1993), 14.
2. Mary Megee, *On Television: Teach the Children,* a video (San Francisco: California Newsreel, 1991).
3. Ibid.
4. Ibid.
5. Ibid.
6. Robert Kubey and Mihaly Csikszentmihalyi, *Television and the Quality of Life: How Viewing Shapes Everyday Experience* (Hillsdale: Lawrence Erlbaum Associates, 1990), 139–144.
7. S. R. Lichter and D. Amundson, "A Day of Television Violence," in *Violence in the Media: An Annotated Bibliography* (Studio City: Mediascope, 1992), 13.
8. R. Caplan, "Violent Program Content in Music Videos," *Journalism Quarterly* 62 (1985): 144–147.
9. Paul Gathercoal, "Brain Research and Mediated Experience: An Interpretation of the Implications for Education," *Clearing House* 63 (February 1990): 271.

10. Ibid., 272.
11. National Coalition on Television Violence, "Rating Cartoons for Violence," in *Congressional Quarterly Researcher* 3, ed. Sandra Stencel (26 March 1993): 172.
12. Jane M. Healy, *Endangered Minds: Why Our Children Don't Think* (New York: Simon and Schuster, 1990), 207.
13. Eugene F. Provenzo, Jr., *Video Kids* (Cambridge: Harvard University Press, 1991), 60–62.
14. Ibid., 33.
15. American Medical Association, *Proceedings of the House of Delegates, June/July 1976* (Chicago: American Medical Association, 1976), 280.
16. Pearl D. Bouthilet and L. Lazar, eds., *Television and Behavior: Ten Years of Scientific Progress and Implications for the Eighties* (Rockville: National Institute of Mental Health, 1982).
17. L. D. Eron and L. R. Huesmann, "The Control of Aggressive Behavior by Changes in Attitudes, Values, and the Conditions of Learning," in *Advances in the Study of Aggression,* eds. R. J. Blanchard and D. C. Blanchard (Orlando: Academic Press, Inc., 1984), 139–171.
18. Aletha C. Huston, et al., *Big World, Small Screen: The Role of Television in American Society* (Lincoln: Nebraska University Press, 1992), 57.
19. *Safeguarding Our Youth: Violence Prevention for Our Nation's Children, Report from the Working Group on Media* (Washington, D.C., July 20–21, 1993), 4.
20. Elizabeth Kolbert, "Study Finds TV Violence on the Rise," *New York Times,* 5 August 1994, A9.
21. *Safeguarding Our Youth: Violence Prevention for Our Nation's Children,* 2.
22. Brandon Centerwall, M.D., "Television and Violence: The Scale of the Problem and Where to Go from Here," *Journal of the American Medical Association* 267 (10 June 1992): 3,059.
23. Ibid.
24. Phil Phillips, *Saturday Morning Mind Control* (Nashville: Oliver-Nelson Books, 1991), 54.
25. Alice Sterling Honig, "Television and the Young Child," *Research in Review* 38 (May 1983): 69–70.

4. The Coin of the Realm: Screen Advertising

1. Ronald K. L. Collins, "Sneakers That Kill: Kids and Conspicuous Consumption," *Media and Values* 52–53 (fall/winter 1990): 7.
2. Joyce Nelson, *The Perfect Machine: Television and the Bomb* (Philadelphia: New Society Publishers, 1992), 69.
3. Victor Strasburger, M.D., *Getting Your Kids to Say "No" in the 90's When You Said "Yes" in the 60's: Survival Notes for Baby Boom Parents* (New York: Simon and Schuster, 1993), 170.
4. G. Comstock and H. J. Paik, "Television and Children: A Review of the Research," *ERIC* document (1987): 33.

5. Jonathan Price, *The Best Thing on TV: Commercials* (New York: Viking, 1978), 112.
6. Charles Johnston and David W. Moore, "Advertising: Art and Artifice," a position paper of The Institute for Creative Development (May 10, 1990): 1.
7. "Selling to Children," *Consumer Reports* (August 1990), 520.
8. Sut Jhally, *Dreamworlds: Sex, Power, Desire in Rock Video,* a video by The Foundation for Media Education (1991).
9. Consumers' Union, *Buy Me That,* a video by Consumers' Union (1991).
10. Robert Cohen, *Insiders' Report: Presentation on Advertising Expenditures* (June 1994): 2.
11. "Material Kids Are on the March," *NEA Today* (April 1994), 10.
12. James U. McNeal, "From Savers to Spenders: How Children Became a Consumer Market," *Media and Values* 52 – 53 (fall/winter 1990): 4.
13. *Advertising Age* (10 February 1992), S20 – S25.
14. Diana M. Zuckerman and Barry S. Zuckerman, "Television's Impact on Children," *Arts in Education* (July/August 1985): 43.
15. Dennis Wharton, "Let 'em Eat Junk? Fat Chance, Solon Says," *Variety* 343 (10 June, 1991): 33.
16. Maurine Doerken, "Classroom Combat: Teaching and Television," *Educational Technology Publication* (1983): 102.
17. "Learning from Television: Commercials Influence Kids," *Media and Values* 59 – 60 (fall 1992): 14.
18. Ibid.
19. Greg Braxton, "Programming 'Specials' Blur Line Further," *Seattle Times,* 16 June 1994, E5.

5. The Show's the Thing! News and Talk Shows

1. Walter Cronkite, "Walter Cronkite on TV," in *Better Viewing: Your Family Guide to Television Worth Watching* (September/October 1994), 7.
2. Stanley Meisler, "Poll: News Media Outclass Churches," *Seattle Times,* 16 March 1994, A5.
3. Martin Lee and Norman Solomon, *Unreliable Sources: A Guide to Detecting Bias in News Media* (New York: Carol Publishing Group, 1990), 16.
4. Neil Postman and Steve Powers, *How to Watch TV News* (New York: Penguin, 1992), 155 – 56.
5. Ron Powers, *The Beast, the Eunuch, and the Glass-Eyed Child: TV in the 80's* (New York: Harcourt-Brace, 1990), 72.
6. Reuven Frank, as quoted by Tom Shales, "Anchors Put On Smiley Faces While the World Has a Bad Day," *Seattle Post-Intelligencer,* 4 August 1993, B6.
7. Neil Postman, *Amusing Ourselves to Death: Public Discourse in the Age of Show Business* (New York: Penguin Books, 1985), 99 – 100.
8. Ibid., 87.

9. Lawrence Kutner, "Television Coverage of Disasters Can Strongly Affect Young Viewer," *New York Times,* 30 January 1994, C11.
10. Arthur J. Deikman, M.D., *The Wrong Way Home: Uncovering the Patterns of Cult Behavior in American Society* (Boston: Beacon Press, 1994), 51.

6. Typecast: Screen Stereotypes

1. Katharine Heintz-Knowles, "The Reflection of the Screen: Television's Image of Children," *Children Now Study* (February 1995), 5.
2. George Gerbner, "Society's Storyteller: How Television Creates the Myths by Which We Live," *Media and Values* 59–60 (fall 1992): 9.
3. Kim Walsh Childers and Jane D. Brown, "Television Viewing and Adolescents' Beliefs About Male-Female Relationships," Association for Education in Journalism and Mass Communication Conference (10–13 August, 1989): 5.
4. Paul Raeburn, "Television's Good Guys Are Lighting Up Again," *Seattle Post-Intelligencer,* 31 October 1993, E4.
5. Bonnie Elson, "Shaping the Minds: Television's Changing Role in Alcohol and Drug Abuse Prevention," *Adolescent Counselor* (June/July 1990), 34.
6. John Murray, "TV in the Classroom: News or Nikes?" *Extra!* 4 (September/October 1991): 6.
7. Narrator, *On Television: Teach the Children,* a video (San Francisco: California Newsreel, 1991).
8. George Gerbner quoted in Mary Megee, *On Television: Teach the Children,* a video (San Francisco: California Newsreel, 1991).
9. Ibid.
10. Betty Miles, *Channeling Children: Sex Stereotyping in Prime-Time TV* (Women on Words and Images, 1975), 23–29.
11. Manuel Mendoza, "Networks Juggling Their Lineups? Try Jiggling Instead," for the *Dallas Morning News* in the *Seattle Times,* 26 July 1994, E8.
12. Diane M. Meehan, *Ladies of the Evening: Women Characters of Prime-Time Television* (Metuchen: Scarecrow Press, Inc., 1983), 109.
13. Eugene F. Provenzo, Jr., *Video Kids* (Cambridge: Harvard University Press, 1991), 108.
14. Childers and Brown, "Television Viewing and Adolescents' Beliefs About Male-Female Relationships," 4.
15. "Sexism on the Superhighway," *Action Agenda* (summer 1994): 5.
16. *Action Agenda* (spring 1994): 8–10.
17. Bernard R. Goldberg, "Television Insults Men, Too," *New York Times,* 14 March 1989, 10.
18. Robert Schrag, *Taming the Wild Tube: A Family's Guide to Television and Video* (Chapel Hill: The University of North Carolina Press, 1990), 68.
19. Ibid.
20. Sally Steenland, "Growing Up in Prime Time: An Analysis of Adolescent Girls on Television," The National Commission on Working Women and Wider Opportunities for Women, 1988.

21. Peggy Charren and Martin Sandler, *Changing Channels* (Reading: Addison Wesley, 1983), 43.
22. Kenney Littlefield, "TV's Age Gap: Young Shows for Older Viewers," *Seattle Times,* 14 August 1994, M8.
23. Ibid.
24. Charren and Sandler, *Changing Channels,* 47–48.
25. Jennifer Sass, *Women Seen on Television,* a video (Portland: The Letting Go Foundation, Inc., 1993).
26. Loring Mandel, "How I'd Save Television," *Parade* (11 May 1986), 11–12.
27. Rick DuBrow, "Prime-Time Portrayal of Latinos Declines," *Seattle Times,* 8 September 1994, F4.
28. Steve Coe, "Cable," *Broadcasting* (13 July 1992), 22–23.
29. Steven A. Seidman, "An Investigation of Sex-Role Stereotyping in Music Videos," *Journal of Broadcasting and Electronic Media* (spring 1992): 214.
30. Petra Hesse, *The World Is a Dangerous Place: Images of the Enemy in Children's Television,* a video (Center for Psychology and Social Change, 1990).
31. Rosalind Bentley, "Black Life on TV Reduced to Rap Beat, Laugh Track," *Seattle Times,* 10 October 1993, F9.
32. Ibid.
33. Ibid.
34. Ann Simonton and Jenai Lane, *Don't Be a TV: Television Victim,* a video (Media Watch, 1993).
35. Conrad Phillip Kottak, *Prime-Time Society: An Anthropological Analysis of Television and Culture* (Belmont: Wadsworth Publishing Company, 1990), 195.
36. Peggy Charren, *Fighting TV Stereotypes* (Reading: Addison-Wesley, 1984), 38.
37. Bruno Bettelheim, "TV Stereotypes 'Devasting' to Young Minds," *U.S. News and World Report* (DATE TK, 1985), 55.
38. Seidman, "An Investigation of Sex-Role Stereotyping in Music Videos," 215.
39. Megee, *On Television: Teach the Children.*
40. Kathleen McCoy, "It's 4 P.M., Do You Know What Your Teens Are Doing?" *Family Circle* (14 May 1991), 54.
41. Jerry Mander, *Four Arguments for the Elimination of Television* (New York: Quill, 1978), 242.
42. Patricia McLaughlin, "Is Mass Media Skewing Our Sense of Beauty?" *Seattle Times,* 6 September 1992, G5.
43. Childers and Brown, "Television Viewing and Adolescents' Beliefs About Male-Female Relationships," 6.
44. David Evans, "The Wrong Examples," *Newsweek* (1 March 1993), 10.
45. Keveney, "Why Does Life on Television Look So Segregated?" *Oregonian,* 5 June 1994, D4.
46. Hesse, *The World Is a Dangerous Place: Images of the Enemy in Children's Television,* 1990.
47. Ibid.
48. Ibid.

Index